Be Prepared!

Guide to Social Audits

Social Compliance with Companies

Jens Schnügger

Book Description:

In order to be well prepared for a social audit, it is important to understand what the supply chain legislation is intended to achieve.

Taking Germany as an example, it can be seen that two different ministries deal with supply chain legislation. One is the Federal Ministry of Labour and Social Affairs (which has an internal impact) and the other is the Federal Ministry for Economic Cooperation and Development (which has an external impact).

It is expected that, just as two federal ministries take care of the various aspects of the law, every company will also take care of these aspects responsibly.

Looking inwards is easier for the vast majority of companies, as these aspects are usually part of their daily work routine. The external view, which includes suppliers, subcontractors and service providers, is more challenging, as it is currently hardly common practice.

This handbook is intended to support companies and managers in the introduction of social standards and to demonstrate a thought structure for this elementary topic so that optimal preparation for the upcoming social audit can take place.

Author Description:

The author Jens Schnügger (MBA), born in Hamburg in 1963, has been advising companies and managers on social sustainability for over 10 years. This includes both social responsibility and social accountability.

Jens Schnügger is also active as a lead auditor for social audits.

The economy is currently in a state of upheaval and greater attention is being paid to the sustainability aspects of supply chains. Sustainability in economic activity has already become established in the structures of companies. However, during his visits to companies, the author repeatedly realises that the important aspect of social sustainability has not yet found its place in the supply chain.

In his book, the author provides the necessary knowledge and background information in condensed form for companies and managers in order to close this gap.

Table of Contents

Foreword

By Audrey Hope

In all my years of being an editor, I have not come across a book such as Well Prepared! Guide to Social Audits that provides such a comprehensive overview of the essential practices and principles related to social audits. It is a valuable resource for anyone who wants to understand how organizations can assess their social impact and performance. This guide effectively transforms complex concepts into understandable language, making it suitable for both professionals and novices in the field. It also covers various aspects of social audits, including their importance, the process of conducting them, and the tools and frameworks available.

One of the outstanding features of this social audits handbook is the inclusion of case studies and real-world examples that help readers connect theory with practical application. These case studies illustrate the positive impact of social audits on organizations and their stakeholders.

Additionally, this book highlights potential challenges and how to effectively address them. It not only provides theoretical knowledge, but also offers step-by-step guidance on planning, conducting, and reporting social audits. The inclusion of templates and checklists adds to the practical nature of the book.

Overall, Well Prepared! Guide to Social Audits is an essential resource for individuals, organizations, and professionals who want to understand, implement, or improve social audit processes. It provides a solid foundation and practical insights, making it a must-read for anyone involved in corporate social responsibility and sustainability.

1

Introduction

The social dimension is becoming more and more important in business life. This is not only happening because so-called predatory capitalism has surpassed itself; rather, legislators and courts have additionally tightened the liability rules for companies.

This book is, therefore, intended as a tool for companies to understand the concept of social sustainability and be prepared for the corresponding audits. The book is not a scientific paper but a sound basis for one's preparation.

Many big corporations require their suppliers to comply with the desired social standards in an explicit fashion.

With SA8000[1], the first comprehensive social standard was developed that was verifiable and that companies could reference.

The challenge with SA8000 was that it could only be passed with 100%, so that the process of certification took a long time.

---

[1] https://sa-intl.org/programs/sa8000/ (Retrieved: 16.AUG.2022)

This approach was suitable in terms of the idea of better embedding the social aspects in companies with increased needs, but it had its limitations when companies wanted to act quickly or when it was applied in areas of the world that already had a good social basis structure.

For this reason, other individually developed standards evolved and with them new business models with which the data of the audited standards became comparable.

To avoid a proliferation of Audit-Standards, companies have joined forces to develop common guidelines and produce comparable results.

Examples are SEDEX[2] (based on the ETI Base Code) or ICS[3] (with its own code of conduct).

Both systems have in common that the audit results are made available to a community of companies, so that an individual company is only audited once and can then refer to the results that have been made available.

This involves each company being audited only once per cycle and agreeing to publish its audit report in the relevant database so that all participating companies can have access to the report.

With the company on site, the audit effort is thus considerably reduced and the clients can additionally use the databases as a sourcing tool to search for further and audited suppliers.

---

[2] https://www.sedex.com/ (Retrieved: 16.AUG.2022)

[3] https://ics-asso.org/ (Retrieved: 16.AUG.2022)

2

Basics

The basic structure of social audits dates back to United Nations General Assembly Resolution 217 A (III) of 10 December 1948, the Universal Declaration of Human Rights and the fundamental conventions of the ILO[4].

"The ILO Governing Body had initially identified eight "fundamental" Conventions, covering subjects that were considered to be fundamental principles and rights at work: freedom of association and the effective recognition of the right to collective bargaining; the elimination of all forms of forced or compulsory labor; the effective abolition of child labor; and the elimination of discrimination in respect of employment and occupation."[5]

The ILO Declaration on Fundamental Principles and Rights at Work (1998) expanded the list to 11 instruments now.

---

[4] https://unric.org/de/allgemeine-erklaerung-menschenrechte/, (Retrieved: 24.JUN.2022)

[5] https://www.ilo.org/global/standards/introduction-to-international-labour-standards/conventions-and-recommendations/lang--en/index.htm , (Retrieved: 30.SEP.2023)

"The eleven fundamental instruments are:

1. Freedom of Association and Protection of the Right to Organise Convention, 1948 (No. 87)

2. Right to Organise and Collective Bargaining Convention, 1949 (No. 98)

3. Forced Labour Convention, 1930 (No. 29)

4. Forced Labour Convention, (its 2014 Protocol)

5. Abolition of Forced Labour Convention, 1957 (No. 105)

6. Minimum Age Convention, 1973 (No. 138)

7. Worst Forms of Child Labour Convention, 1999 (No. 182)

8. Equal Remuneration Convention, 1951 (No. 100)

9. Discrimination (Employment and Occupation) Convention, 1958 (No. 111)

10. Occupational Safety and Health Convention, 1981 (No. 155)

11. Promotional Framework for Occupational Safety and Health Convention, 2006 (No. 187)"[6]

In addition, DIN ISO 26000 was introduced, which refers to the 17 UN goals. The International Organization for Standardization (ISO) defines:[7]

"For businesses and organizations committed to operating in a socially responsible way, there's ISO 26000.

It provides guidance to those who recognize that respect for society and the environment is a critical success factor. As well as being the "right thing" to do, the application of ISO 26000 is increasingly viewed as a way of assessing an organization's commitment to sustainability and its overall performance.

ISO 26000:2010 provides guidance rather than requirements, so it cannot be certified to unlike some other well-known ISO standards. Instead, it helps clarify what social responsibility is, helps businesses and organizations translate principles

---

[6] https://www.ilo.org/global/standards/introduction-to-international-labour-standards/conventions-and-recommendations/lang--en/index.htm , (Retrieved: 30.SEP.2023)

[7] https://www.iso.org/iso-26000-social-responsibility.html (Retrieved, 22.SEP.2023)

into effective actions and shares best practices relating to social responsibility, globally. It is aimed at all types of organizations regardless of their activity, size or location."

The UN describes the stated goals as follows:

"The Sustainable Development Goals are vital for a recovery that leads to greener, more inclusive economies, and stronger, more resilient societies."[8]

"The Sustainable Development Goals are the blueprint to achieve a better and more sustainable future for all. They address the global challenges we face, including those related to poverty, inequality, climate change, environmental degradation, peace and justice."[9]

The Sustainable Development Goals goals are[10]:

Goal 1: End poverty in all its forms everywhere (No Poverty)

Goal 2: Zero Hunger

Goal 3: Ensure healthy lives and promote well-being for all at all ages (Good Health and Well-Being)

Goal 4: Quality education

Goal 5: Achieve gender equality and empower all women and girls (Gender Equality)

Goal 6: Ensure access to water and sanitation for all (Clean Water and Sanitation)

Goal 7: Ensure access to affordable, reliable, sustainable and modern energy (Affordable and Clean Energy)

Goal 8: Promote inclusive and sustainable economic growth, employment and decent work for all (Decent Work and Economic Growth)

---

[8] https://www.un.org/sustainabledevelopment/sdgs-framework-for-covid-19-recovery/ (Retrieved, 22.SEP.2023)

[9] https://www.un.org/sustainabledevelopment/%20sustainable-development-goals/ (Retrieved, 22.SEP.2023)

[10] https://www.un.org/sustainabledevelopment/%20sustainable-development-goals/ (Retrieved, 22.SEP.2023)

Goal 9: Build resilient infrastructure, promote sustainable industrialization and foster innovation (Industries, Innovation and Infrastructure)

Goal 10: Reduce inequality within and among countries (Reduced Inequalities)

Goal 11: Make cities inclusive, safe, resilient and sustainable (Sustainable Cities and Communities)

Goal 12: Ensure sustainable consumption and production patterns (responsible Consumption and Production)

Goal 13: Take urgent action to combat climate change and its impacts (Climate Action)

Goal 14: Conserve and sustainably use the oceans, seas and marine resources (Life Below Water)

Goal 15: Sustainably manage forests, combat desertification, halt and reverse land degradation, halt biodiversity loss (Life on Land)

Goal 16: Promote just, peaceful and inclusive societies (Peace, Justice and Strong Institutions)

Goal 17: Revitalize the global partnership for sustainable development (Partnerships for the Goals)

As complex as this list may seem, a picture will emerge in the further work that will form an audit framework.

3

The ESG Framework

The three letters ESG stand for the following areas:

- Environment

- Social

- Governance (corporate management) and their significance for voluntarily sustainable corporate behavior. The focal points are spread across the following topics:

Corporate governance, compliance, occupational safety, working conditions and environment.

Prior to discussing the individual topics, we look at the subject as a whole and ask ourselves: What is the intention of this?

The years 2012 and 2013 were particularly traumatic for Bangladesh. On 24 November 2012, a fire broke out in the "Tazreen Fashion"[11] garment factory and then on 24 April 2013, Rana Plaza[12] burned down. It was found that the buyers

---

[11] https://cleanclothes.org/campaigns/past/tazreen (Retrieved, 30.SEP.2023)

[12] https://www.publiceye.ch/de/themen/mode/gesundheit-sicherheit-arbeitsplatz/bangladesch/rana-plaza (Retrieved, 30.SEP.2023)

were more concerned about production costs than the safety of the labor force working in the factory.

The following indignation among customers led to a rethinking, which led to the textile industry being the first sector to develop a social standard. This resulted in SA 8000, the first robust auditing standard.

The subsequent outcry among customers led to a change in thinking, which resulted in the textile industry being the first industry to develop a social standard. This development resulted in the SA 8000 as the first resilient testing standard.

Other industries claimed that their suppliers had better conditions and therefore did not have to have a social standard.

This situation has changed. Social standards are gradually gaining acceptance in all sectors.

2021, the world's first Corporate Due Diligence Act was passed in Germany.

The responsible Federal Ministry for Economic Cooperation and Development states:[13]

> *"The globalization of economic cycles has resulted in companies moving many parts of their production processes overseas. For instance, a T-shirt travels on average 18,000 kilometers before it ends up in a shop in Germany.*
>
> *Some 80 per cent of worldwide trade now relies on global supply chains, which provide a livelihood for more than 450 million people."*

And continues:

> *"In order to better protect human rights along global supply chains, for instance, by preventing child and forced labor and banning substances that are harmful to humans and the environment, the German government adopted the Act on Corporate Due Diligence Obligations for the Prevention of Human Rights Violations in Supply Chains (also known as the supply chain law)."*

---

[13] https://www.bmz.de/en/issues/supply-chains (Retrieved, 30.SEP.2023)

The Federal Cabinet launched the bill on March 3 (2021). The Bundestag passed the bill on June 11, 2021. The Bundesrat approved the law on June 25, 2021.[14]

"The aim of this law is to improve the protection of human rights and the environment in global supply chains. The aim is not to implement German social standards everywhere in the world, but to ensure compliance with fundamental human rights standards, such as the ban on child labor and forced labor, and key environmental standards, such as the ban on the contamination of drinking water. Companies in Germany also bear responsibility for this. They must ensure that human rights and environmental standards are respected in their supply chains. The law lays down clear and implementable requirements for companies' due diligence obligations and creates legal certainty for companies and those affected."[15]

A law for fair supply chains - what is that all about?

Again, the Federal Ministry for Economic Cooperation and Development provides the necessary clarifications:

"Central regulations:

1. Clear requirements for corporate due diligence for the first time.

   Creating legal certainty for companies and stakeholders.

2. Responsibility for the entire supply chain.

   The due diligence obligations of companies basically cover the entire supply chain - from the raw material to the finished product on sale.

   The requirements for companies are differentiated, in particular, according to the degree of influence on the perpetrator of the human rights violation or environmental pollution, as well as according to the different levels in the supply chain. Companies must take action if there are clear indications of violations.

---

[14] Excerpt at Chapter 11
[15] https://www.bmz.de/de/themen/lieferkettengesetz (german page) (Retrieved, 22.SEP.2023)

3. External verification by an authority

   The Federal Office of Economics and Export Control (BAFA), an established authority, verifies compliance with the law.

   BAFA monitors company reports and investigates complaints submitted. If the BAFA notes any omissions or violations, it can impose fines or exclude companies from public procurement.

4. Better protection of human rights

   Those affected by human rights violations can continue to assert their rights in German courts and can now also file complaints with the Federal Office of Economics and Export Control."[16]

Why is this regulatory framework so important?

Germany is home to multinational companies. The automotive sector, in particular, has a global impact on supply chains.

If the major automotive manufacturers and the largest suppliers act in unison, this has a global impact on the diverse locations of the suppliers.

The advantage of the Supply Chain Act is that all companies are treated equally. The disadvantage is that the check lists have to be designed in a way that they can cover all countries and so some check points need to be interpreted somehow differently in different countries.

Another disadvantage is that only a snapshot can be taken at one time, be it remotely, on-site, or even just data-based.

Today, it can be noted that corporations are delegating their obligations arising from the Supply Chain Act to their supplier factories.

This makes it important for each individual company to be prepared. This book is intended to be a cornerstone for that preparation.

---

[16] https://www.bmz.de/de/themen/lieferkettengesetz (german page) (Retrieved, 22.SEP.2023)

3.1 Benefits for companies (external)

This book addresses those entrepreneurs who consider employees as production factors.

All production factors require regular maintenance, which is why this book is intended for entrepreneurs who see employees as production factors. In order to maintain productivity, machines have a maintenance schedule; employees need rest periods and vacations.

That payment is sufficient (and thus above minimum wage or defined "living wage") is evidently presupposed in this book.

It is true that some companies see their employees only as cost factors and are intent on keeping production costs low.

For many entrepreneurs, an upcoming social audit is an additional burden where they, somewhat reluctantly, have to spend time with the auditor and answer questions whose meaning they do not understand.

However, with some preparation, many companies can gain beneficial ideas from these audits.

What are the external benefits of a social audit?

1. You stay listed with your customer.
2. The audit systems such as **SEDEX** and **ICS** work with databases where members can access the status of each audited company. This opens up the possibility for you to gain new customers.
3. The audit result can be used for marketing measures, e.g. as a competitive differentiation.
4. The audit can help you with **ESG** reporting requirements.

The Supply Chain Act (Gesetz über die unternehmerischen Sorgfaltspflichten zur Vermeidung von Menschenrechtsverletzungen in Lieferketten

(Lieferkettensorgfaltspflichtengesetz, LkSG, short form: Supply Chain Act)[17] requires companies that are affected by the Act to review the supply chain for social minimum standards.

At the time of writing this guide, many companies had their own standards (e.g. Amazon, Home Depot, Costco or Zalando).

While other companies have joined an alliance.

At ICS[18], among others: Adeo, Auchan RETAIL, Carrefour, Club Med, Galeries Lafayette or Maison du Monde.

At SEDEX[19] you will find, among others: Anheuser - Busch, ASDA, McLaren Automotive, METRO AG, Miller Coors, Mondelez or Nestle.

The advantage of SEDEX and ICS is obvious: the audit burden on the individual suppliers is reduced and after passing or failing the audit, all member companies have the right to access the result.

Note to colleagues from purchasing departments reading this:

Your company's internal Code of Conduct requires you to ensure that minimum social standards are met.

The system of paying bonuses when clear savings are achieved has logical limits.

If you charge purchase prices that cause the contractor's employees to slip below the minimum wage, you are not fulfilling the obligation, according to your own code of conduct.

---

[17] https://www.bmz.de/de/themen/lieferkettengesetz/ (Retrieved, 14.SEP.2023)

[18] https://ics-asso.org/our-members/ (Retrieved, 22.SEP.2023)

[19] https://www.sedex.com/about-us/our-members/ (Retrieved, 14.SEP.2023)

3.2 Benefits for companies (internal)

The benefits for the clients are clear, they secure their supply chain, but what are the benefits for the audited companies?

At first glance, business leaders in Western Europe say they don't understand why they are being audited and point the finger at other regions of the world.

Then, after the audit, most managers note that there is room for improvement after all.

This is just a preliminary remark to show that all companies can learn from the audits and that there is always dormant potential to be leveraged.

It is an undisputed fact that the potential is greater in some regions of the world than in others.

The focus of the audits is on governance, compliance, occupational health and safety, and the environment.

Looking only at the topics, every company manager and executive will say that there are no problems with these topics in their own company.

This is a healthy and confident attitude, but as the saying goes, "The devil is in the details."

This applies especially to the audit areas in the companies, where it depends again and again on the little things.

This means that companies learn from each audit where processes and procedures can and should be readjusted to put the company in a better position. This applies in particular to the company's own employees: Satisfied employees work more effectively than dissatisfied ones, but it is clear that each person defines his or her level of satisfaction individually.

It is the task of management to set the best possible framework conditions, thus giving employees the best possible starting position.

This implies that companies will learn from each audit where processes and procedures can and should be readjusted in order to improve the company's position. This is especially true for the company's own employees: Satisfied employees work more effectively than dissatisfied ones, but it is clear that each person defines their level of satisfaction individually for himself or herself.

It is the responsibility of management to set the best possible framework conditions, thus giving employees the best possible starting position.

When considering the production factor "human being", it is therefore important to design the work environment in such a way that employees feel comfortable. A company benefits directly from this, because it is still true that good employees do not complain, they leave the company.

Management's other important task is, therefore, to prevent internal resignation and to retain employees, which will then definitely prove to be an advantage.

This is particularly true in regions where the change of generations means that there is a shortage of skilled workers, and therefore, every employee should be kept on as long as possible.

In regions where there are no problems with the availability of new employees, it is nevertheless important to set up the company in such a way that an excessively high turnover rate is prevented, because high turnover increases costs, such as process costs (e.g., induction costs and training time).

If the employees do not feel the need to move to another company, the work process will become more favorable in the long run due to decreasing overhead costs, which is an advantage that every company manager would like to experience.

3.3 Governance

Germany's "Gabler Wirtschaftslexikon" defines governance as: "Corporate governance refers to the legal and factual regulatory framework for the management and supervision of a company."[20]

And further, it is stated:

"Corporate governance regulations basically have the task of limiting the scope and motivations of actors for opportunistic behavior by means of suitable legal and de facto arrangements."

The definition of governance from the Oxford Advanced Learner's Dictionary is[21]:

"The activity of governing a country or controlling a company or an organization; the way in which a country is governed or a company or institution is controlled."

In the policy note of the Committee for Development Policy of the United Nations, "Global governance and global rules for development in the post-2015 era[22]", principles for reform are identified.

Five focus areas are defined as examples[23]:

- Shared but differentiated responsibilities according to respective capabilities.

- The principle of subsidiarity

- Inclusion, transparency, accountability

- Coherence and

- Responsible sovereignty

Some may ask why the UN is being referred to in this context and what the relevance of this to the company is.

The topics apply analogously in companies.

---

[20] https://wirtschaftslexikon.gabler.de/definition/corporate-governance-28617#head7 (Retrieved: 24. JUL. 2022)

[21] https://www.oxfordlearnersdictionaries.com/definition/english/governance (Retrieved, 30.SEP.2023)

[22] Global governance and global rules for development in the post-2015 era, United Nations publication. Sales No. E.14.II.A.1, ISBN 978-92-1-104689-2, eISBN 978-92-1-056769-5, Copyright @ United Nations, 2014.

[23] Global governance and global rules for development in the post-2015 era, p.28ff.

Common, but differentiated, responsibilities: according to the individual capabilities imply: How is the company management organized, how are the tasks assigned, and is each position occupied by the best possible person? Or do reassignments in that way make sense in that they advance the company?

The principle of subsidiarity/decentralization: Does the CEO have to be in charge of all decisions or can tasks be better allocated and can or should decisions then be made at the departmental level, and what parameters then need to be set?

In addition, the supplier sector also has to be taken into account here: Do your suppliers/subcontractors comply with all the specified requirements? To be investigated in this case would be: Compliance with minimum wage or living wage, working conditions, and contractual regulations, etc. Does this sound familiar?

You are about to have a social audit because these basic principles, passed on to you by your customer, are to be checked at your company. The following rule applies here: Customers must ensure that their suppliers/subcontractors are complying with all the relevant regulations.

In the end, this implies that you need to ensure compliance with the rules by your suppliers, i.e. the next level(s), by conducting social audits (or an equivalent).

The wording of the law requires the entire supply chain![24]

Inclusivity, transparency, responsibility/accountability:

Inclusion (from Latin inclusio, "inclusiveness, enclosure" and "the fact of including somebody/something; the fact of being included"[25]): How do you include people? At the company, this refers to the principle of freedom of association and the principle of collective bargaining.[26]

---

[24] https://www.gesetze-im-internet.de/lksg/ (Retrieved: 10.JUN.2023)

[25] https://www.oxfordlearnersdictionaries.com/definition/english/inclusion?q=inclusion (Retrieved: 301.OCT..2023)

[26] https://www.ilo.org/berlin/arbeits-und-standards/kernarbeitsnormen/lang--de/index.htm (Retrieved: 24. JUL. 2022)

Transparency: This refers to the company's uniformity of contracts and their use and implementation.

Accountability: This refers to the Accountability of corporate Responsibility (e.g., compliance with social standards in the supply chain, verified, for instance, through social audits).

Coherence (the situation in which all the parts of something fit together well[27]) refers to the consistency or solidarity within the company; in this context, it refers to discrimination, bullying and/or abuse.

The UN report describes **responsible sovereignty** as "necessary for the efficient provision of global public goods, for managing interdependence, and for achieving global sustainable development." [28]In terms of the company, this is about managing resources and the environment in broader terms.

3.4 Compliance

Compliance is described as adherence to laws, rules and standards.[29] For companies, this means checking whether all the relevant legal principles are being observed or the practice of obeying rules or requests made by people in authority.[30]

DIN ISO 37301[31] is defined as follows:

1. Compliance: Fulfillment of all compliance obligations of the organization

2. Compliance culture: Values, ethical principles, beliefs, and behaviors that exist within an organization and interact with the organization's structures and control systems to create standards of behavior conducive to compliance.

3. Compliance function: A person or group of persons with responsibility and authority for the operation of the compliance management system.

---

[27] https://www.oxfordlearnersdictionaries.com/definition/english/coherence (Retrieved: 30. SEP9. 2023)

[28] Global governance and global rules for development in the post-2015 era, p.30

[29] ttps://wirtschaftslexikon.gabler.de/definition/compliance-27721#:~:text=Definition%3A%20Was%20ist%20%22Compliance%22,von%20Gesetzen%2C%20Regeln%20und%20Normen. (Retrieved: 14.JUN.2023)

[30] https://www.oxfordlearnersdictionaries.com/definition/english/compliance?q=compliance (Retrieved: 01.OCT.2023)

[31] INTERNATIONAL STANDARD, ISO 37301, First Edition 2021-04, Compliance Management Systems

4. Compliance risk: The likelihood of occurrence and the consequences of non-compliance with the organization's compliance obligations, and additionally,

5. Behavior: Behaviors and practices that impact outcomes for customers, employees, suppliers, markets and communities.

Compliance is therefore used to depict an overarching topic in which the legal landscape of the company is reviewed.

For example: Which legal requirements must be met in order to operate the company, including the commercial/trade register, legal register (in order to stay up to date with the applicable laws) and labor law principles.

Although in the field of governance, it is reviewed how and with which implementation the company is managed, in the area of compliance, attention is paid to adherence to the legal framework. In this context, the supplier/subcontracting companies are also included in the assessment. This is important because suppliers' behavior can cause compliance problems for the company itself.

An example could be that the utilization of chemicals causes environmental damage (or even personal injury) at your supplier company, which falls back on you as the ordering party because you have demanded this chemical utilization.

This fall back does not necessarily mean financially, but rather, the possible image risk is meant as a relevant risk factor, and this cannot be contractually excluded. These occur spontaneously and are considered to be „entrepreneurial risk"! Because you have selected the supplier/subcontractor.

Supplier companies are subjected to an ethical audit to mitigate this risk.

As additional scopes, traceability and transparency are checked here:

- In production, products and batches must be traceable.

- All documents and requested records must be transparent.

3.5 Occupational safety and Hygiene

Occupational Health and Safety is a sub-topic of Compliance that follows its own guidelines.

On the one hand, a safe working environment is imperative for employees. On the other hand, there are defined hygiene requirements to be met, e.g. cleanliness at the workplace, cleanliness/hygiene around toilets, washrooms and changing rooms, and where employees take their meals.

In any given country, there are regulations that map and regulate the topic of occupational health and safety. If in doubt, the ILO regulations on occupational health and safety should be referenced[32] :

- Sanitation (Trade and Commerce) Convention, 1964 (No. 120).
- Occupational Safety and Health Convention, 1981 (No. 155).
- Occupational Health Services Convention, 1985 (No. 161).
- Occupational Safety and Health Promotion Framework Convention, 2006 (No. 187).

There is additionally ISO 45001:2018: Occupational health and safety management systems.

ISO describes the concept on its website as follows:[33]

"ISO 45001:2018 specifies requirements for an occupational health and safety (OH&S) management system, and gives guidance for its use, to enable organizations to provide safe and healthy workplaces by preventing work-related injury and ill health, as well as by proactively improving its OH&S performance."

And later:

"ISO 45001:2018 can be used in whole or in part to systematically improve

---

[32] https://www.ilo.org/global/standards/subjects-covered-by-international-labour-standards/occupational-safety-and-health/lang--en/index.htm (Retrieved: 10.JUN.2023)

[33] ttps://www.iso.org/iso-45001-occupational-health-and-safety.html, (Retrieved: 08.JUN.2023)

occupational health and safety management. However, claims of conformity to this document are not acceptable unless all its requirements are incorporated into an organization's OH&S management system and fulfilled without exclusion."

The occupational health and safety section is an imminent part of a social audit and any step that will improve the working environment of the workforce is to be appreciated. Just the presence of a certificate does not imply that the working conditions are good, but it is an indicator of the company's will to create the best possible working environment.

3.6 Environment

Any business activity has an impact on the environment, which is why a sustainability audit that fails to take environmental factors into account makes no sense.

In various audit catalogs, there are a number of different ways of approaching the environment, ranging from a brief overview to extensive environmental audits.

What is at stake?

In an atmosphere where climate aspects are becoming more and more important, and customers are also paying more and more attention to CO_2 footprints and the avoidance of (plastic) waste, it is important for companies to know how their own supply chain is organized and where potential risks are to be expected.

While not all business activities can be implemented without risk to the environment, this increases the importance of knowing the potential hazards.

For example, there is a high demand for dyeing mills in the textile industry. It is well known that the dyeing mills are working with potentially hazardous substances. For the risk assessment of the supply chain, it is essential to know which substances are used and in what quantities. Do they have their own effluent treatment plants or how is the wastewater situation locally managed?

Likewise, it is useful to know to what extent electricity is obtained from renewable energy sources and from which origins, or why not.

Inversely, the question arises with the audited company, why am I obliged to provide this data?

This is more about the implication of "dealing with the issue."

Many companies know their energy demand and consumption that is indisputable. By questioning this data, the focus is automatically directed back to consumption and sources of supply, and companies are beginning to look at potential savings.

With many entities taking many small steps towards savings and improvements, this automatically leads to a reduction in the environmental burden.

This scenario applies likewise to the quantities of waste that are generated in companies.

Broadening the perspective in this regard:

1. What types of waste are generated?
2. How is the waste disposed of? Recycling or landfill?
3. Is it possible to trace how waste is treated if it is disposed of via third parties?

The objective in this context is to ensure that the environment is not polluted more than absolutely necessary.

The first questions focused on land and air: Let's look at noise.

When a company is built "on a greenfield site," villages are usually created in the surrounding area because employees want to live in the immediate vicinity of the workplace. In addition, there are retail stores that cover people's daily needs.

At this point, at the very latest, the company is faced with the question of potential noise pollution. It is, therefore, important to know what noise emissions are emitted by the company's own processes.

Biodiversity is a further area of concern. The company seals surfaces.

Can these plots of land be compensated? What are the company's possibilities for minimizing the direct impact on the environment?

At this point, it is obvious why these audits are called "sustainability audits" - the situation beyond the actual production process is audited.

With these audits, employees and the environment are converted from cost factors to production factors, which are then subject to a different consideration compared to cost factors. The company becomes aware that it benefits from a sustainable approach to employees and the environment and, ideally, companies start to focus more on sustainability aspects of all kinds.

A further aspect to be considered is the change of perspective on the environment.

What influences does or can the environment have on your company? A classic example of this is the location along a river:

Initial situation: Your plant is located on a river, you process chemicals and you use the river as a transport route.

Several questions then come to the fore, relying on your risk management. What can happen if the river:

a. Overflows its banks during high water or

b. Even runs dry during low water?

How are you prepared? How are the emergency chains organized? Etc.

There are similar questions if, for example, the plant being inspected is located in a mountainous area.

In this case, rock fall and accessibility would be added as consideration scenarios.

4

Customer requirement: Social /Sustainability audit

Your company has gained a large, international company as a customer. You are proud of this, but then you are told: "Before we can call off the first delivery, you are required to have a social audit. The audit standard we accept is: "xyz." To make things easier for you, we have prepared a piece of paper so that everyone can have information and find possible audit companies."

Now it is up to you to look for a service provider who is able and authorized to assess the requested standard.

Ideally, you will get an agenda and an overview of the information that will be requested during the audit and prepare for the audit date.

However, as usual, things don't always go so smoothly, and the audit will be exciting for you...

Likewise, the consultant who usually assists you in the certifications has not been able to gain enough experience so far to support you through the upcoming ethics audit, and the audit date is approaching.

In this situation, it is, therefore, a matter of keeping calm and preparing as reasonably as possible.

4.1 Code of Conduct

One cornerstone of the audit is the code of conduct. In many cases, companies have little to do with the term "code of conduct."

The "Wirtschaftslexikon Gabler"[34] defines the Code of Conduct as "a collection of guidelines and/or regulations which companies impose on themselves as part of a voluntary self-commitment. The formulated behavioral instructions serve as a (basic) action orientation for employees in order to channel desired behavior or to avoid undesired actions. In terms of subject matter, the set of rules can be very broad and range from corruption to dealings with customers to working time regulations, and the level of detail can also vary greatly. Often part of CSR strategies."

And the Cambridge Dictionary states: "a set of rules that members of an organization or people with a particular job or position must follow[35]."

In Germany, there is the Government Commission on the German Corporate Governance Code[36], which draws up a code for companies listed in the German stock indices independently of the government.

For most mid-sized companies, the proposed framework outlined here is too complex and does not fit their existing structures.

---

[34] https://wirtschaftslexikon.gabler.de/definition/code-conduct-51600/version-274761 Code of Conduct revision dated 02/19/2018 - 15:09 (Retrieved: 24.MAR2023).

[35] https://dictionary.cambridge.org/dictionary/english/code-of-conduct (Retrieved: 01.OCT.2023)

[36] https://dcgk.de/de/ (in English: https://dcgk.de/en/home.html) (Retrieved: 24.MAR.2023)

A customized, tailored framework could, for example, include the following points:

4.1.1 Definition of the core values of the company

1. On which ethical principles do you base your activities?

2. Do both employees and business partners are aware of these principles?

3. Are the principles mandatory and can all stakeholders refer to these fundamental principles? And how?

4.1.2 Corporate Governance

1. Are the rules that you have set yourself implemented?

2. What are the possibilities for responding to infringements?

Internally:

1. How does the company respond to violations by employees?

2. How can employees report violations by the company?

Externally:

1. Are all stakeholders aware of the code of conduct?

2. How does the company react to violations by stakeholders?

3. How can stakeholders react to violations committed by your company?

4.1.3 Social Togetherness

1. How do companies and their employees interact with each other?

2. What does the Charter of the UN Human Rights[25] regulate?

3. How are these rules implemented in the company?

4. Are there local laws? (E.g. in Germany the General Equal Treatment Act (AGG)).

5. How do companies interact with each other?

4.1.4 Sustainable and ecological behavior

1. What is the definition of sustainability?

2. Is a definition of social sustainability available?

3. Does a definition exist for ecological sustainability?

These are the questions that provide a framework in which management sets the rules that govern its own company.

These rules are individually defined, as each management can and will have its own individual approach.

The most important rule is: The Code of Conduct must fit the company, not the company to the Code of Conduct.

4.1.5 Codes of conduct in implementation

As inspiration, various codes from companies of different sizes and from different industries are listed here.

Beiersdorf[37]	Constantia Flexibles[38]
Volkswagen[39]	AS Creation[40]
BlackRock[41]	Ankerkraut[42]
Vion[43]	Heckler & Koch[44]
Carrefour[45]	Nolte[46]
Wacker Chemie[47]	Freeze Dry Foods[48]
Sainsbury's[49]	McLaren[50]

---

[37] https://www.beiersdorf.com/investor-relations/compliance/code-of-conduct (Retrieved: 15.JUN.2023)

[38] https://www.cflex.com/general-terms-conditions/code-of-conduct/ (Retrieved: 15.JUN.2023)

[39] https://www.volkswagen-group.com/de/publikationen/weitere/code-of-conduct-1882 (Retrieved: 15.JUN.2023)

[40] https://www.as-creation.com/unternehmen/ueber-uns/compliance/code-of-conduct (Retrieved: 15.JUN.2023)

[41] https://www.blackrock.com/corporate/responsibility/ethics-and-integrity (Retrieved: 15.JUN.2023)

[42] https://www.ankerkraut.de/pages/nachhaltigkeit (Retrieved: 15.JUN.2023)

[43] https://www.vionfoodgroup.com/en/our-responsibility/ (Retrieved: 15.JUN.2023)

[44] https://www.heckler-koch.com/de/Unternehmen/Compliance (Retrieved: 15.JUN.2023)

[45] https://www.carrefour.com/en/csr/responsible-conduct (Retrieved: 06/15/2023)

[46] https://www.nolte.de/compliance.html (Retrieved: 15.JUN.2023)

[47] https://www.wacker.com/cms/de-de/about-wacker/wacker-at-a-glance/corporate-strategy-and-policy-guidelines/ethical-principles.html (Retrieved: 15.JUN.2023)

[48] https://www.freeze-dry-foods.com/nachhaltigkeit (Retrieved: 15.JUN.2023)

[49] https://www.about.sainsburys.co.uk/sustainability/better-for-everyone/human-rights (Retrieved: 15.JUN.2023)

[50] https://group.mclaren.com/group/news/articles/code-of-conduct-and-business-ethics/ (Retrieved: 15.JUN.2023)

4.2 A quick solution must be found

The two major audit concepts: ICS and SEDEX/SMETA, both offer preparation documents. Simply visit the appropriate website, download the information, and off you go.

Unfavorably, the information is written in a very rudimentary, or to put it more kindly, global way, because no one wants to be left holding the bag.

Still, the quick fix is:

4.2.1 Preparation for the scope of inspection

1. Find out which standard you are to be audited against.

2. If a customer-specific questionnaire is required, criteria are usually available for this questionnaire, according to which the audit is conducted. Ask for these basics!

3. Review topics and compile documents that fit the topic, because it is better to be half-prepared than not to be prepared at all.

4. When requesting an audit, there is usually a contact person at your customer who is responsible for the audit (sometimes even a separate department); try to obtain further information.

Internally, deal with the following topics in advance:

4.2.1.1 Occupational health and safety

1. What are the possible occupational safety risks to be considered in the company?

For example:

- Chemical hazards
- Physical hazards
- Biological hazards
- Ergonomic hazards
- Psychological hazards

2. Are all risk assessments available?

4.2.1.2 Document review

Are all required permits, approvals, and/or authorizations copies on file? Mandatory documents are the company's own Code of Conduct and approval as a business enterprise (e.g., extract from the Trade Register).

4.2.1.3 Preparatory Work / Organization

Assure that the HR department is manned on the day of the audit and that access (access rights must be guaranteed) to all data and documents is possible.

One note concerning the above: Many audits are only conducted as "semi-announced," for which a time window is advised. Make sure that days when you cannot guarantee the audit have been communicated to the auditing company.

If not all documents are available at the audit, it will be difficult. Documents that cannot be audited will be noted as nonconformance.

If you have temporary personnel, inform the recruitment agencies that personnel data of temporary workers will be requested.

Temp agencies often refuse to provide access to the data, citing data protection issues. One option is to have the release of the data guaranteed in your master agreement. For example, by formulations such as: "In the event of a social audit, the temporary employment agency will provide the requested data. Data protection is granted," whereby this formulation is only intended as an example and does not develop any legally binding force.

The intention here is to indicate that each company must, in advance, come to an agreement with its service providers on the provision of documents. How or which solution they find is up to the individual situation; the only important thing is that the access is made possible.

In general, we can assume that you will have the appropriate signature for this purpose, because the employees will be asked to release their personal data.

Note: No data will be processed. Personal data are considered as the only relevant documentation in order to verify data and to make possible falsifications and deceptions more difficult.

At the time of writing, the first companies have started to use the non-supply of documents as a trigger for blocking deliveries.

Ensuring decent working conditions is a top priority in this context and is applied globally on a generalized basis.

4.2.2 Proverb: "The wise man makes provisions for the future."

The best option is to look for literature on the market that will help you prepare.

You probably won't find literature that covers all the issues, because that would completely miss the point.

In the same way, there is no "always fits" situation for ISO 9001, because every company is different. A management system will only make sense if it fits the company.

On the contrary, fitting the company to the management system, in the end, will not work because processes that are practiced will not be covered by the system.

When preparing for a social audit, it is similar: topics are questioned, but each company may take different approaches in order to meet various challenges and requirements.

This involves checking your management handbook and figuring out where and how each of the requirements can be built into the system.

The better the requirements are linked to your company's own management system, the easier it will be for you to get through the upcoming social audits.

The most important rule is: If you cannot reflect some core elements, you can expect a re-audit. In the worst case, you will lose a customer.

Why is that?

Because it is difficult for the customer to ensure that their supply chain complies with legal requirements.

And this has nothing to do with the quality of the delivered products! - It is all about compliance!

5

A Leadership and Guidance Framework

First of all, A social audit is hardly rocket science!

Contrary to the "normal" audits, not the process, but the employees are the focus of the assessment.

All questions primarily focus on the employees and their status within the company.

It is evident that the usual master data are requested, but subsequently, the topics focus on the working relationships and the focal point is the employee.

Do not treat any group of questions casually!

Even if you are convinced that the legal situation in your surroundings prohibits child labor or forced labor, face the questions and examine your processes!

Social auditors undergo a training process designed by APSCA[51] – Association of Professional Social Compliance Auditors to ensure worldwide consistency in auditor standards.

---

[51] https://www.theapsca.org/ (Retrieved: 16.AUG.2022)

This implies that any accredited auditor can theoretically conduct audits in any country in the world and according to uniform criteria.

Local auditors know the intricacies of local legal situations better than colleagues from outside, but this does not exclude the possibility that you may be audited by an auditor from another country.

Working with colleagues from other countries, as in a training course, always ensures that auditors question their own procedures. Through this and through daily practice, the auditors learn and can adapt or react to the respective situations on site.

5.1 Individual preparations

Apart from the basic structures listed in Chapter 4, how can you prepare for a social audit?

1. Preparation of the basic data of the company
2. Are you a single company or part of a group of companies?
3. What data do you have in-house or what data, if any, are organized centrally?
4. If you are part of a group of companies: Make sure they have access to central functions on the day of the audit.
5. If you are a sole proprietor: Ensure that departments are staffed so that all access rights are available.
6. If you have outsourced any sub-tasks to third parties (tax advisor, external HR department), ensure that the most important information is in-house or, if necessary, can be passed on.
7. Inform recruitment agencies and service providers that data may be requested from them, refer to supply chain laws.

Please keep in mind that audits are always spot-checks, so there is no single solution as to what further data is required.

In the auditing process, it may happen that one track is followed more intensively than another; this is up to the auditor and arises from the situation on site.

5.2 Structured Preparation

A structured preparation would be, if you explicitly take care of the social audit and develop a folder and an audit structure for it, as you do it with your preparations for ISO audits.

Use your customer's criteria as a basis for this.

Since the audit topics of the social audit are interrelated and are nevertheless examined from different perspectives, you can, for example, use the structure of the Balanced Score Card.

6

A Balanced Score Card

What is a Balanced Scorecard (BSC)?

Prof. Dr. Dr. h.c. Jürgen Weber defines[52]: "The Balanced Scorecard is a link between strategy development and implementation. In its concept, traditional financial metrics are supplemented by a customer perspective, an internal process perspective, and a learning and development perspective."

The BSC is a system for measuring a company's performance, using such things as customer satisfaction, employee knowledge, and the company's use of new ideas[53].

In the balanced scorecard concept, traditional financial metrics are supplemented by a customer perspective, an internal process perspective, and a learning and development perspective.

Norton and Kaplan have thus added a learning curve, or feedback loop, to the system of strict metrics.

---

[52] https://wirtschaftslexikon.gabler.de/definition/balanced-scorecard-28000/version-251640
Revision von Balanced Scorecard vom 20.02.2018 - 17:04 (Retrieved: 26.DEC2022)
[53] https://dictionary.cambridge.org/dictionary/english/balanced-scorecard (Retrieved: 01.OCT2023)

It is indisputable that other systems are used in the subject area of strategic planning and that the Balanced Scorecard has a disadvantage in some areas of application. For our purposes, the underlying structure for strategy is a reasonable starting point, as it is about a jump start.

6.1 Development of a Balanced Social Scorecard (BSS)

In the traditional strategy map, the four starting points: Customer, Finance, Learning & Growing and Internal Processes are cross-linked via checkpoints.

For the Balanced Social Scorecard, the initial structure is used and the four benchmark levels are renamed to Social, Environment, Legal and Corporate.

If one now falls back on the environmental factors and the ETI base code, the result is a complex network that would be better represented as a sphere, since the various topics interact with each other.

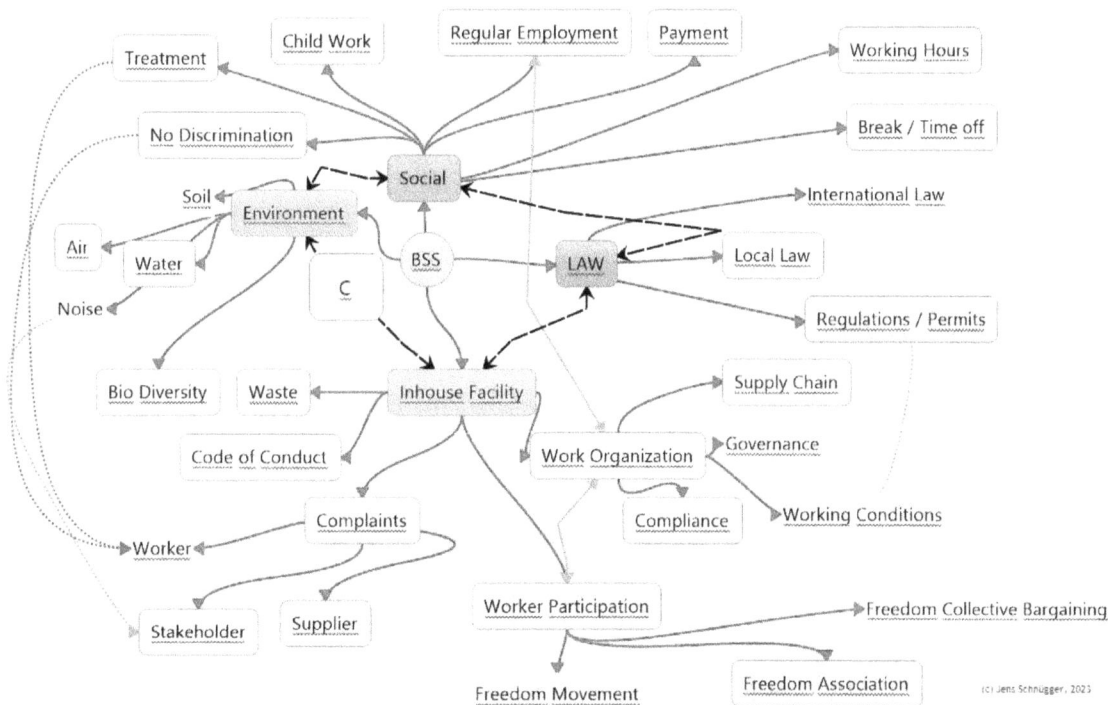

Figure 01: Interrelationships in the structure of a Balanced Social Scorecard

It can be seen in the picture that levels interact: here exemplary:

1) "[humane] Treatment" and "No Discrimination" link to Complaints/Worker → as there is the complaint function for employees here.

2) Environment / Noise links to Complaints / Shareholders → this is where residents can complain about noise emissions from the company.

3) For example, there is a link „Regular Employment" to „Work Organization" and

4) "Worker Participaion" → the first part deals with the use of temporary workers and the second deals with the workers' right to participate.

5) The last example links "Regulation / Permits" to "Working Conditions" - the compliance of working conditions with legal requirements.

6.2 BSS: An approach

The strategic approach to preparing for a social audit is for the relevant management team to look at the basics of a social audit and then to review the current implementation in their own company.

6.2.1 SEDEX / SMETA / ETI Base Code

The most convenient starting point is to check the implementation of the ETI Base Code (see Chapter 9).

"In January 1998, a small number of British retailers, aid agencies, workers' rights organizations and trade unions come together to promote fundamental human rights in global supply chains. Subsequently, under the pivotal leadership of Secretary of State for International Development Clare Short, ETI is incorporated as a not-for-profit company on 9th June. We receive start-up grants from the Department for International Development and the Department of Trade and Industry.

From the very start, corporate, NGO and trade union members agree that for ETI to be successful, they must collaborate to identify and promote good practice.

Our tripartite approach is born."[54]

The 9 clauses of the ETI Basic Code are[55]:

1. Employment is freely chosen:

   Slavery and forced labor are totally unacceptable. Approximately 12.3 million people worldwide are forced to work for their employers.

2. Freedom of association and the right to collective bargaining are respected:

   Tens of thousands of workers lose their jobs every year for trying to join a union or improve working conditions. Some even lose their lives.

3. Working conditions are safe and sanitary:

   Every day, 6,000 people worldwide die from work-related accidents or illnesses. Most of these tragedies could be prevented.

4. Child labor must not be used:

   218 million children work to support their families, missing out on education and often harming their health. This exacerbates the cycle of poverty.

5. Living wages are paid:

   3 billion of the world's poor live on less than two dollars a day. When people cannot support their families on an adult's wage, they may send their children to work.

6. Working hours are not excessive:

   Long hours are the norm for most workers in the world. This harms people's health and undermines family life.

7. Discrimination is not practiced:

   Women and certain minorities are often confined to the lowest-paying jobs and do not have access to training or promotion.

---

8. Regular employment is guaranteed:

   Most workers can be fired when it suits the employer. This fuels poverty and insecurity and depresses wages.

9. No harsh or inhumane treatment is allowed:

   Few workers are protected from physical, verbal or sexual violence in the workplace.

If a self-confident manager looks at the nine headings, he will presumably say:

"No problem, we cover everything."

It is only at second and third glance that the shoals in these waters come to light, and a somewhat more in-depth study will lead to a result similar to the example in Fig. 1.

Each company must define for itself how the sub-areas "social," "environment," "legal" and "corporate" interact.

There is no standard solution. In each country, there are different legal foundations, e.g. the legal foundations for pay regulations in Austria and Germany are fundamentally different, and the use of temporary workers in Taiwan is different from that in the USA.

It is precisely this disparity that can be overcome in the audit, and thus, companies in all countries become comparable, despite all the legal differences.

6.3 The ICS Systematic

On its website and in the manual for factories, the ICS describes itself as follows:

"ICS is a France-based initiative created in 1998 by the FCD, Fédération Française du Commerce et de la Distribution, so celebrating its twentieth year in 2018!"[56] This makes 25 years in 2023.

---

[56] https://ics-asso.org/our-story/ (Retrieved, 01.OCT.2023)

ICS member brands and retailers have worked together since its foundation to sustainably improve conditions for people at work, and responsibly support their supplying factories to implement progress and compliance. ICS enables its member companies to collaborate with common tools, to mutualize audits, contributing to the reduction of the 'audit fatigue' and share knowledge and best practices.

This joint approach is guided by the framework defined by the International Labour Organization (ILO) conventions, the universal Human rights principles and local social regulations. ICS members verify the actual working conditions in their supplying production sites by mandating ICS-accredited audit companies to conduct social audits. After the assessment, ICS members engage with the audited factories to implement the defined corrective action plans.

This system is, therefore, designed to ensure that audit reports can be viewed in a database by all member companies and that existing results can be used as a foundation.

The fact that a large number of industries have agreed on one (or two, as there is a separate environmental questionnaire) also implies that all companies are audited according to a uniform questionnaire. This increases comparability.

ICS Code of Conduct

Each ICS member requires its suppliers to comply with the ICS Code of Conduct, which may be supplemented by the member's own detailed Code of Conduct.

By signing this Code, the supplier undertakes to conform to it and to obtain from his own subcontractors and partners that they also commit to it.[57]

Shared responsibility is a key concept.

---

[57] ICS Social Code of Conduct, Version 2018, Download 01.OCT.2023

The Code of Conduct covers the topics:

➢ Chap. 0 - Management system, transparency and traceability.

➢ Chap. 1 - Minimum age, child labor and young workers

➢ Chap. 2 - Forced labor

➢ Chap. 3 - Non-Discrimination

➢ Chap. 4 - Disciplinary practices, harassment and abuses

➢ Chap. 5 - Freedom of association and grievance mechanisms

➢ Chap. 6 - Working Hours and Overtime

➢ Chap. 7 - Remuneration and Benefits

➢ Chap. 8 - Health and Safety

"ICS actions are based on shared tools and a common methodology applied by all ICS members and securing a complete control of the audit process by brands.

- ICS Social and Environmental Code of Conduct defines the core requirements that suppliers must commit to.

- Before being audited, the factory fills-in the ICS Factory Profile notably with production site data and the list of production processes undertaken internally and externally. This declaration helps ICS members for the mapping of their supply chains.

- The cornerstone of the ICS system is the audit report questionnaire used in 65 countries.

- After the completion of the audit, the factories and the ICS members work on the Corrective Action Plan (CAP) recommended by the auditor."[58]

---

[58] https://ics-asso.org/our-tools/ (Retrieved, 01.OCT.2023)

7

Develop a Strategy, Key Figures and Audit Points

In order to properly prepare for the audit, the first thing to do is to check individually in each company which topics are interrelated and how.

This is illustrated by the following diagram.

Based on this visualization, a start can be made to develop a structured approach.

It is important to note that this visualization is not a definitive statement, but is intended to provide food for thoughts.

For the key figures and check figures that follow, the ETI Base Code is used as a guideline for the determination of the components.

Figure 02: Basic Components

		HSE	Contractor	Worker	Job	Money	HR	Management System	
		**Key Indicators, Social Audits**							
Management System	Code of Conduct	Environment							Fire Safety & Accidents
		Emergency Exit				Collective Bargaining			
		Emergency Pathways						Stakeholder Management	
HR			Complaint System				Written Contract		
					Min. Wage				
			Contract Language				Proper Contract details		
					Living Wage				
			Proper Contract details				Contract Language		
			Bonus Scheme						
Money			Proper Payment				Payment Concept		
Job		Machine Safety			Job Promotion		Job Description		
			Overtime						
		E-Safety				Job Cluster			
			Working Hours						
		Workspace Safety				Gender Dependent			
			Rest Breaks						
Worker			Workers Committee						
							Contact Possibility		
			Union					Recruitment Abroad	
Contractor				Recruitment Fee					
			Sub-Contracting				Written Contract		
				Debt Scheme					
			Out-scourcing				Proper Contract details		
							Contract Language		
HSE					Waste Handling				
			HSE Committee					Accidents	
	© Jens Schnuegger, 2023	Dormitory							

42

7.1 Key Performance Indicators

Before we talk about possible key performance indicators, a fundamental point needs to be clarified with regard to the key performance indicators used: Key performance indicators for the sake of it don't make sense, because they have to make sense and they have to have a message.

A key performance indicator could be:

$$Correct\ Payment = \frac{Number\ of\ Employees\ receiving\ at\ least\ minimum\ Wage}{Number\ of\ contracted\ Employees}$$

Figure 03: Example KPI

The question is, is this a useful figure?

In order to make this figure meaningful, the current wage or minimum wage would have to be available for each individual employee. In addition, the number of employees would have to be a) defined and b) available. If these values are available, the result is only a YES or NO.

Whereby "No" as a result is not good.

A problem in this context could be, for example, the apprentices. If you calculate their salary by the hours, you will get values below the minimum wage. On the other hand, it is possible that the salary of the apprentices is set by external institutions.

And in addition, it must be explained: What is meant by "contractually bound"? Does this include the temporary workers, for example, because they are bound to the company by a framework agreement?

The obvious shortcoming is: there seem to be people who are not contractually bound. So it would be necessary to check what are the constructs behind these people.

This means that every key performance indicator necessarily needs to be carefully thought through before it is used.

7.2 Framework values

Key Indicators, Social Audits									
		HSE	Contractor	Worker	Job	Money	HR	Managment System	
Managment System	Code of Conduct	Environment							Fire Safety & Accidents
HR									
Money									
Job									
Worker									
Contractor									
HSE									
© Jens Schnuegger, 2023		Dormitory							

Figure 04: Framework Values

With the framework perspectives, it is important to note that they affect all perspectives. In the subtopics, partial aspects of the framework perspectives are always considered, so that the perspectives are always considered where it is appropriate to do so.

Basic values (framework values):

1) Code of Conduct Yes / No → If No: Develop Code of Conduct.

2) Environment:

   2.1 Are all legal principles known?

   2.2 What influences does the company have on the environment?

   2.3 What influences does the environment have on the company?

   2.4 How can third parties raise complaints?

   2.5 How is the complaint response organized?

   2.6 What training is required for employees?

3) Fire and accidents:

   2.1. What fire safety measures have been taken?

   22 Are accidents recorded?

   23 Are accidents analyzed and preventive measures taken?

4) Employee accommodations

   4.1 Are accommodations provided? Yes / No

   4.2 If yes: Have all checkpoints been checked, as they are in the company?

   4.3 If not all test points have been tested: Why not?

7.2.1 Assignment and generation of key performance indicators

It is known from the Balanced Scorecard and the Strategy Map that the various key performance indicators are assigned to the different perspectives.

The perspectives in this case deviate significantly from the familiar structures, so that the renaming to a Balanced Social Scorecard (BSS) makes sense.

The following perspectives have been defined for the BSS in the above diagram (see page 33):

Management System, Human Resources, Worker, Contractor, Health & Safety, Money, Job.

And as framework perspectives:

Code of Conduct, Environment, Fire Safety & Accidents, and Dormitory.

On the basis of the graphic "theme affiliation", the following test values are considered:

Basically, there are values that are fixed: YES = 1 and NO = 0.

If a value is less than 1, an increased risk for the employees can potentially be derived from this.

A "correct" key performance indicator is not always necessary, especially if the questions require a "yes/no" answer.

7.2.2 Code of Conduct

The Code of Conduct defines the relationship between the company and its employees and the environment, as well as the intended relationship between employees

These guidelines are specific to the company and provide the compass for the audit. The company's organization is based on the provisions defined in the Code of Conduct, as they are derived from the company's philosophy.

- Does the company have its own Code of Conduct? Yes / No If yes: Does it include all necessary points?

- Is there a requirement from your customer to publish the customer code of conduct? Yes / No

- If yes:

    • Where / how was it published?

    • Has any training been provided on this? When? Any repeats? Has the Code of Conduct been understood?

$$Code\ of\ Conduct = \frac{Own\ Content}{Content\ Requirements}$$

Figure 05: Content of Code of Conduct

Please note that your Code of Conduct regulates the relationship with your suppliers/subcontractors in the same way.

This indicates that you are required to check/ensure compliance with the specified guidelines at your supplying companies/subcontracting companies.

$$Third-Party\ Effect\ of\ Code\ of\ Conduct = \frac{Situation\ at\ the\ Supplier}{Content\ Requirements}$$

Figure 06: External impact of the Code of Conduct

If you are currently conducting supplier audits at your supplier factories, these must be expanded to include the contents of your Code of Conduct.

If you do not conduct on-site audits, a verifiable proof must be provided by the supplier company.

For you this has the following implications:

1) Checking your own specifications in the Code of Conduct

2) Checking at the supplier company (among other aspects for :)

2.1) Wages / Salaries

2.2) Working Hours

2.3) Occupational Health and Safety

2.4) Discrimination / Bullying

2.5) Abusive use of temporary workers

2.6) Subcontractors (if applicable, also to be checked there)

Thus, everything that your customer expects from you, you must ensure or check with your subcontractors. It is up to you whether you have this checked by your own personnel or by third parties.

A governance approach is always derived from the code of conduct.

$$Governance = \frac{Implementation\ in\ the\ Company}{Content\ Requirements}$$

Figure 07: Behavioral Guidelines from the Code of Conduct

This may look straightforward, but all the sub-aspects need to be considered here too.

For example: Home office: do you use Microsoft Teams in-house, for example? (This may apply to any other software solution)

- Have employees created their own groups?

- Are external persons in these groups?

- What access do the external persons have to the company system (if applicable, were rights assigned and not revoked again)?

- Have groups been dissolved or do they currently exist?

- Do these groups form entry gates for third parties?

7.2.3 Environment

The Environment category is concerned, on the one hand, with environmental influences caused by the company and, on the other hand, with the influences that the environment has on the company.

Influences on the environment can be, for example, noise or air emissions.

Influences by the environment can arise, for instance, from a location on the water (risk of flooding) or from a remote location (risk of accessibility).

At this point, each company must individually determine for itself which potential hazards it is dealing with.

- How is responsibility governed?

- Are there any official or legal requirements? Yes / No

- If yes: Are all requirements known?

- What are the requirements?

- Is there a list of requirements?

- Are all requirements up to date?

- Are all internal procedures up to date?

- Is there an environmental certification?

- Is there a biodiversity policy?

- Are all the company's impacts on the environment known?

- CO^2 footprint

- Noise emissions

- Water/groundwater hazards?

7.2.4 Fire Safety & Accidents

Fire Safety & Accidents is all about the organizational view of fire safety and (possible) accidents.

For the following points, what is the organizational framework?

7.2.4.1 Emergency exits

Occupational Health and Safety is one of the most important requirements. Sufficient and accessible emergency exits must be available.

$$Emergency\ Exit = \frac{(Distance * (Value\ On\ Opposite\ Side) * (Value\ Illuminated) * (Value\ Accessible) * (Value\ Accessibility)}{Number\ of\ Emergency\ Exits}$$

Figure 08: View of emergency exits

Or:

$$Emergency\ Exit\ [Value > 1?] = \frac{(Value\ [2] * (Value\ [3]) * (Value\ [4]) * (Value\ [5]) * (Value\ [6])}{Value[1]}$$

Figure 09: Emergency exits under consideration

This Key Performance Indicator consists of different Sub-Values for which the following parameters are to be used:

Value 1: Number of existing emergency exits (fixed value)

Value 2: Distance between emergency exits (legal value)

$$Distance = (legal\ requirement) - (measured\ distance)$$

Figure 10: Distance between emergency exits

Value 3: Emergency exits located opposite each other. Are there opposite emergency exits? Yes/No

Value 4: Lighting of emergency exits

- Is emergency lighting provided for each emergency exit? Yes/No

- Is the existing lighting in function? Yes/No

- If No: For how many emergency exits is the lighting inoperative?

$$Lighting = (Value\ Existing) * \frac{Number\ of\ Defective\ Lighting}{Number\ of\ Emergency\ Exits}$$

Figure 11: Lighting at emergency exits

Value 5: Accessibility (legal requirements)

Are all necessary legal requirements in place? (Yes/No)

Detailed check: What are the requirements for emergency exits? (e.g. steps, door opening, opening mechanism)

Are there any exceptional circumstances?

$$\begin{aligned} &Accessibility \\ &= (Value\ Legal)) \\ &* \frac{(Number\ of\ Problematic\ Emergency\ Exits - (\frac{Number\ of\ Problematic\ Emergency\ Exits}{Number\ of\ Existing\ Exemptions})}{Number\ of\ Emergency\ Exits} \end{aligned}$$

Figure 12: Accessibility / Reachability of Emergency Exits

or:

$$(Number\ of\ Problematic\ Emergency\ Exits) - \left(\frac{Number\ of\ Problematic\ Emergency\ Exits}{Number\ of\ Existing\ Exemptions}\right) = Accessibility$$

Figure 13: Accessibility / Reachability of Emergency Exits

Value 6: Accessibility

Are all escape routes free of obstructions? Yes/No

Only after checking the data at this point, a value can be determined.

7.2.4.2 Escape routes

The term "escape routes" refers to the paths leading to emergency exits.

First and foremost, the legal requirements must be respected here, and this should be a straightforward matter, of course.

In addition, it should be checked whether your customer, who is demanding the audit, has specific, more detailed requirements.

$$Escape\ Routes = \frac{Legal\ Requirements + Specific\ Requirements}{Number\ of\ Escape\ Routes}$$

Figure 14: Evaluation of escape routes

This formula may appear, at first glance, an easy one to solve. On a more detailed look, it can lead to problematic issues.

1) Do you have an overview of the legal requirements?

2) Are you aware of customer-specific requirements?

If yes for both questions: How is the update organized?

7.2.4.3 Accidents

Accidents are among the incidents in working life that can always occur and that need to be prevented.

The primary objective is, therefore, to make sure proper documentation is in place:

1) Are accidents recorded?

2) Are accidents categorized?

3) What categories are in use?

4) Are accidents analyzed and prevention strategies developed?

5) How are accidents and strategies documented and how is it tracked?

6) Are accident statistics kept?

$$Accident\ Rate = \frac{Accidents}{Number\ of\ Employees}$$

Figure 15: Calculation of Accident Rate

$$Accident\ Rate\ Production = \frac{Accidents\ Production}{Number\ of\ Employees\ Production}$$

Figure 16: Calculation of Accident Rate in Production

$$Accident\ Rate\ Serious\ Accidents$$
$$= \frac{Accidents\ Resulting\ in\ Fatality + Accidents\ Resulting\ in\ Body\ Injuries}{Number\ of\ Accidents}$$

Figure 17: Calculation of Accident Rate with Serious Consequences

7.2.4.4 Dormitory

Do you provide housing or dormitories for employees? Have all labor law checkpoints been investigated for this subsection?

The ETI Base Code requires in item 3.4: "Accommodation, where provided, shall be clean, safe, and meet the basic needs of the workers."

For each accommodation, it must be individually verified that emergency exits, escape routes, first aid, fire protection, etc. have been properly implemented.

$$Accomodation = \frac{Check\ Points\ (HSE + Contractor + Worker + Job + Money + HR + Management\ System)}{Number\ Accomodation\ [Dormitory]}$$

Figure 18: Dormitory Safety

In accommodations, employees are also subject to hazards because they rely on the security organized by the company.

Have all the checkpoints that apply internally to the company also been checked for the accommodations?

The records of the respective inspections are required for this purpose.

7.3 Topic-specific

Chart 02 has specified the topics "Environment", "Fire Safety", "Employee Accommodation" and "Code of Conduct" as framework areas, as these reach into all areas.

The subdivisions in detail revolve around the topics: "Management System",

"Human Resources", "Compensation", "Workplace", "Employees", "Service Providers and Subcontractors", and "Occupational Health and Safety".

Since the breakdown is schematic, each area is linked to each level. This leads to similar topics being questioned at different stages.

7.3.1 Management system

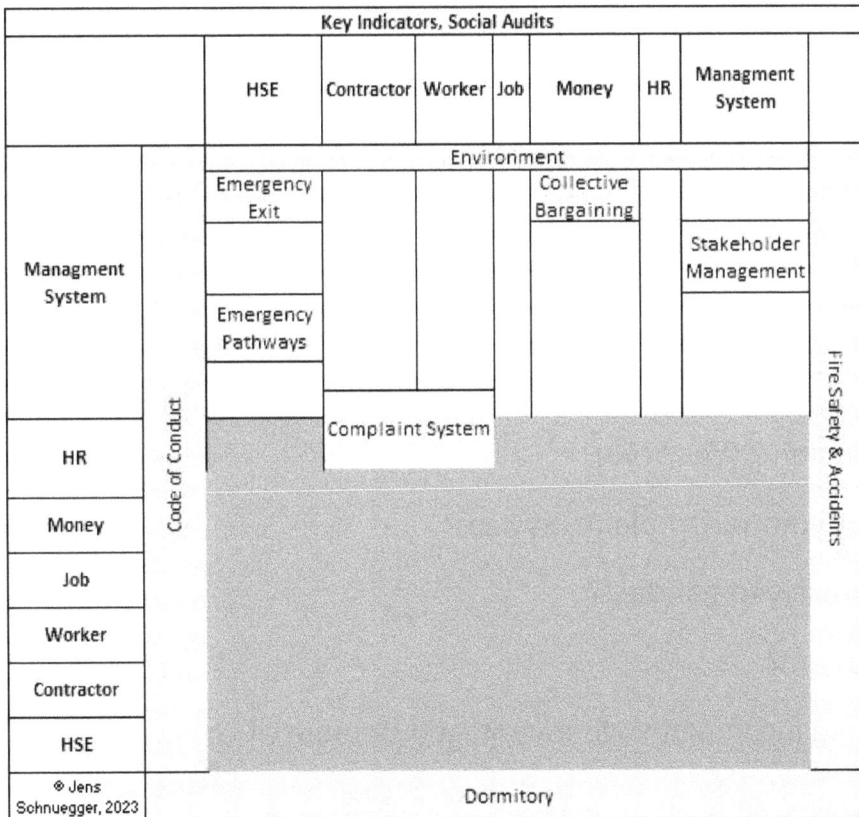

Figure 19: Important test points for the management system

This area focuses on organizational issues.

The ETI Base Code does not set any specific requirements for management systems, but at the same time, a management system is indisputable as a regulatory tool. In the diagram above, four thematic blocks form a framework, as they influence all sub-areas.

The management system is not defined as a framework element in this approach, as it is created on a company-specific basis and the Code of Conduct provides the framework for the management system.

The diagram indicates that separate organizational considerations should be made for the sub-areas of Occupational Health and Safety/Environment, Service Providers, Employees, Workplace, Compensation, and Personnel. The organization has a great deal of this data, but additively, it should add to the following items:

1) Emergency exits and escape routes were covered above (item 7.2.3.1f / page 42f).

2) Complaint management system: In this paper, only the interrelationships between service providers and employees are discussed. Third parties and the supply chain must also be taken into account.

Checkpoints can be:

1) Is there a complaint system? (Yes / No)

2) If yes: Is there an anonymous complaints system?

3) How are complaints received handled?

4) Is there a feedback system?

5) Are employees who file a complaint disadvantaged because of complaints?

6) How is this data recorded and how is access governed?

7) Is the data treated confidentially?

There is no Key Performance Indicator for this; rather, the procedure is checked by following up on a case.

a) When was the complaint received?

b) What was the exact procedure for the complaint?

c) How and at what point was there consultation with the departments concerned?

d) How was the feedback from (c) dealt with? Did any new insights emerge from it?

e) What was the feedback like?

f) What was learned from the process and how were the results used for improvement?

From a broader perspective, there is an item called "Collective Bargaining"; there are several sub-items considered under this review topic:

Freedom of Assembly and Freedom of Bargaining.

The EIT Base Code, under its Topic 2, is defined as follows:

"Freedom of association and the right to collective bargaining are respected".

1) Are workers allowed to organize?

2) What is the legal framework?

3) Is there any impediment to organizing?

3) Are employees penalized (financially, transfer, dismissal) for wanting to organize?

4) Is there a collective bargaining agreement?

5) If not, what are the pay structures?

6) How is it ensured that equal pay is paid for equal work?

Another point to consider is the checkpoint named in the chart: stakeholder management.

Here, it is necessary to examine:

1) Which parties may have a legitimate interest in the company's work? Examples: Investors, NGOs government agencies, press

2) How is the interaction organized?

3) Are there designated contact persons?

4) What are the competencies of these contact persons?

5) Is the communication documented?

6) What benefits could be derived from the dialogue?

Point number seven of the EIT Base Code requires:

"No discrimination is practiced."

The management system must, therefore, regulate how discrimination is prevented at all levels.

$$Discrimination = \frac{(Desired\ Behaviour + Training + Publications)}{Awareness\ Among\ Employees}$$

Figure 20: Discrimination in the company

Point number nine of the ETI Base Code additionally requires:

"No harsh or inhumane treatment is allowed."

Therefore, the audit of the complaint systems additionally examines what the provisions are in the case of bullying and harassment and how corresponding indications are dealt with.

$$Inhumane\ Treatment = \frac{(Desired\ Behaviour + Training + Publications) * Complaint\ Channel}{Awareness\ Among\ Employees}$$

Figure 21: Inhumane Treatment

Furthermore, the existing complaints procedure is also considered:

$$Complaint\ Possibility = \frac{Anonymous\ Complaint\ Channel * Open\ Complaint\ Channel}{Awareness\ Among\ Employees}$$

Figure 22: Complaint procedure

7.3.2 Human Resources

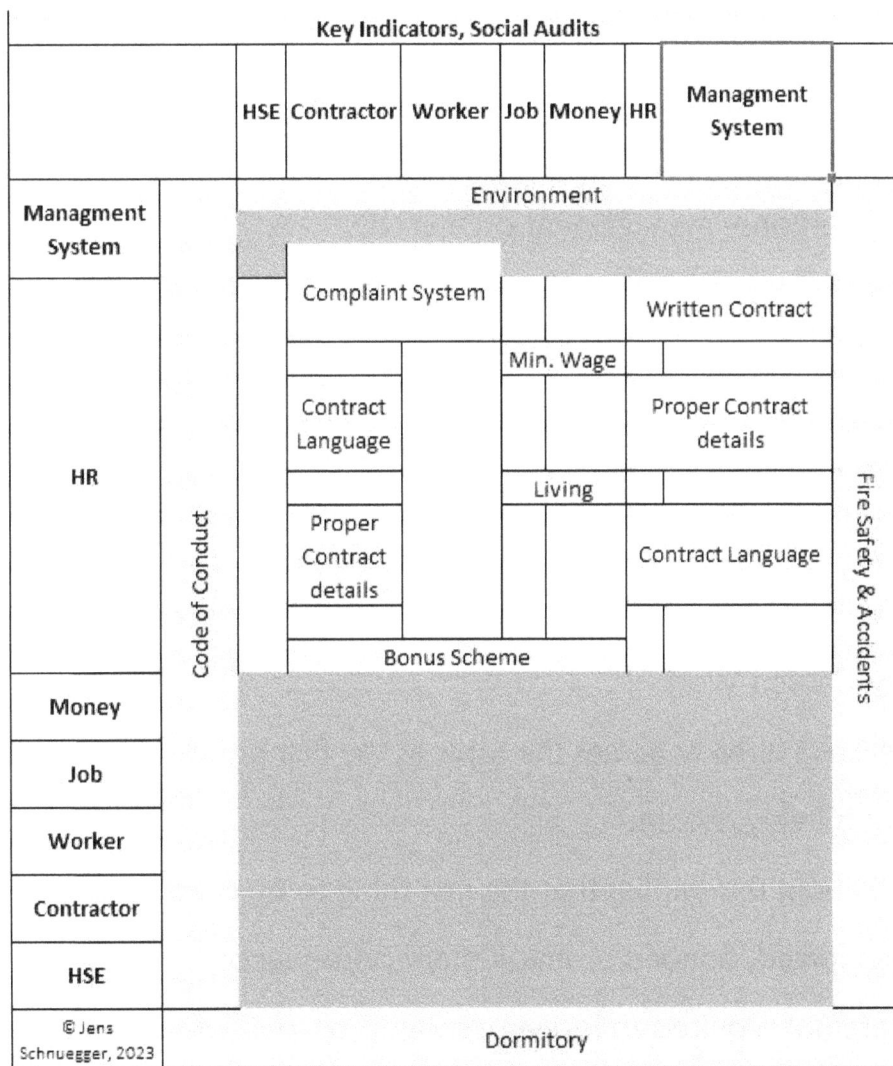

Figure 23: Important Checkpoints within the HumanResources Department.

How do the exemplary topics mentioned in the diagram interact with each other?

Prior to entering into the detailed evaluation, a few fundamental questions need to be addressed:

1) Is the management of the personnel carried out by a responsible and competent department?

2) Is there a personnel department? Is this internal or external?

3) If the HR department is external: - Do the employees have contact persons? And how can they be contacted?

- Are there office hours?

- How can employees submit questions?

- How is the response management organized?

The basic idea behind these queries is that, in the event of problems, employees must be able to obtain qualified information. If „only" the managing director can answer questions, it must be critically examined whether an employee can actually trust that the information is correct and whether questions can be asked without the risk of being dismissed.

7.3.2.1 Freely Chosen Work

The ETI Base Code already names the topic as the first point:

"Employment is freely chosen."

In its interpretation, this implies that the first thing to be checked is:

- There is no forced, bonded or involuntary prison labor.

- Workers are not required to lodge "deposits" or their identity papers with their employer and are free to leave their employer after reasonable notice.

In many companies, this requirement is often faced with a lack of understanding, as they cannot imagine why this should be checked and the above points seem self-evident.

It should be remembered that each country has a different approach to employment relationships and that what applies in A-country is by no means valid in B-country.

The fact that the topic has its own sensitivity can be illustrated using the example of the United Kingdom.

In the UK, the Modern Slavery Act 2015[59] is in effect, and every company with a business location in the UK is audited against this Act.

The draft bill was introduced in the House of Commons in October 2013 by James Brokenshire, the parliamentary under-secretary of state for crime and security. He was quoted as saying that the bill would "send the clearest possible message to criminals that if they are involved in this disgusting human trafficking, they will be arrested, prosecuted and imprisoned."[60]

This seems to be a big sledgehammer to crack a nut; but that is exactly what it is not!

It is rather easy to apply the law, or its intentions, to daily life.

Examples:

1) Is a maid paid with cash? Consequences:

    a) Obvious: Both parties save taxes (but legally: tax dodging).

    b) Long-term consequence: The maid thereby does not pay into the pension funds and thus runs the risk of being subject to old-age poverty.

2) A Romanian welder is hired in Western Europe and receives the local minimum wage. Since the welder wants to earn a lot of money quickly, he works double shifts and/or 7 days straight - the company he works for agrees to this behavior.

---

[59] https://www.legislation.gov.uk/ukpga/2015/30/contents/enacted (Retrieved: 08.JUN.2023)
[60] https://en.wikipedia.org/wiki/Modern_Slavery_Act_2015 Retrieved: 08.JUN.2023)

Possible effects:

  a) Little rest time affects work results: poor performance, regress.

  b) The person in question overexploits his body and the risk of accidents is increased.

  c) After an accident, he is not further employed by his company and is supposed to return "home." The "how" is left up to him (and "of course" at his own expense!!).

  d) In not all cases, the hours are fully compensated after the termination of the employment. In this case, presumed local laws and regulations are used, which the employee cannot comprehend (The document found locally, which is the basis of this example, caused amazement during the audit ...).

Third example:

3) Cleaning staff: the staff is paid according to the collective bargaining agreement, but at least minimum wage.

So far, no problem can be identified.

  a) The quantity of the surface to be cleaned, with the same time default, is increased. This means that, in effect, the cleaning area is paid less than the minimum wage (either legally or according to the collective agreement).

  b) The time requirements for the same area size are reduced, so that less time per area is available for cleaning. This approach may also result in undercutting the minimum wage.

4) Last example: Contracts for work with a unit limit.

A contractor awards a contract for work with a number of units to be produced.

The contractor calculates the quantity to be produced and deploys a corresponding number of employees at the applicable minimum wage.

Over a longer period of time, additional work is performed: on the one hand, because the client increases the number of units and, on the other hand, because the contractor does not provide any additional employees.

If, however, each individual employee now has to perform more work, the minimum wage is effectively undercut because more work has to be performed in the same period of time.

To make things clearer, the specification is, for example, that each person must manage 400 items per hour. Due to an increase in orders, the working persons are now supposed to create 450 pieces (this corresponds to 12.5% more work, which is not compensated by more money (this is only temporary...).

Not always where the minimum wage is written on it, the minimum wage is in it! -- Pay attention to the nuances!

For auditors, the phrase of Chremes[61] applies: "Homo sum, humani nihil a me alienum puto." Translated: "I am a human: I regard nothing human as foreign to me."

Not all cases are always obvious.

How would you, as a reader, judge the following situation?

Once a year, an employee and his or her supervisor have an appraisal meeting. During the interview, the employee's work performance is evaluated. The supervisor refuses to give a good grade with the reason that the employee does not work overtime.

---

[61] Heauton Timorumenos by Terenz

The following questions arise:

1) The employee manages his workload without working overtime. Why is this not being graded?

2) If overtime is voluntary, why is there criticism about the lack of overtime?

3) What will be achieved with the statement? The employee is being devalued, his work performance is not being recognized and he will explicitly not apply for overtime anymore. (This was the case in the audited case).

4) However, if the employee gives in, what can happen?

This is where the ETI Base Code must be considered, which states in section 6.3:

"All overtime shall be voluntary. Overtime shall be used responsibly, taking into account all the following: the extent, frequency and hours worked by individual workers and the workforce as a whole. It shall not be used to replace regular employment. Overtime shall always be compensated at a premium rate, which is recommended to be not less than 125% of the regular rate of pay."

So the answer to the above question must be:

Forced labor exists because in order to receive a good evaluation, the employee must work overtime.

"Bonded labor" is another point of consideration.

Bonded labor means that employees have to work in a company for a defined period of time because, for example, they have to meet payment obligations or they had to hand over ID documents.

What is thereby meant are funds, where one cannot avoid to spend them, in order to be able to take up the work.

Example:

An employee from country A would like to take a job in country B. In order to get the job, he turns to an intermediary agency, which provides him, a passport, visa, job, work permit and accommodation, for a fee.

The intermediary grants a credit, which the employee can only work off by being bound to a defined minimum term of the contract.

In particular, the first chapter of the ETI Base Code applies here:

1. Employment is freely chosen

> 1.1 There is no forced, bonded or involuntary prison labor.
>
> 1.2 Workers are not required to lodge "deposits" or their identity papers with their employer and are free to leave their employer after reasonable notice.

7.3.2.2 Child Labor

Chapter four of the ETI Base Code defines:

4. Child labor shall not be used

> 4.1 There shall be no new recruitment of child labor.
>
> 4.2 Companies shall develop or participate in and contribute to policies and programmes which provide for the transition of any child found to be performing child labour to enable her or him to attend and remain in quality education until no longer a child; "child" and "child labour" being defined in the appendices.
>
> 4.3 Children and young persons under 18 shall not be employed at night or in hazardous conditions.
>
> 4.4 These policies and procedures shall conform to the provisions of the relevant ILO standards.

An age check must therefore be made in all employment contracts. In addition, it must be checked how the company prevents child labor from taking place.

Age at Start of Work $>=$ Minimum Age

Figure 24: Minimum Age Check

Have a list be generated displaying all employees who have not reached the age of 18 yrs. to the current date.

For each of these individuals, verify the date of birth and the date they joined the company.

Age at Start of Work $=$ Entry Date $-$ Date of Birth

Figure 25: Check Child Labor

Minimum result: >14 years (local legal requirement if applicable) → The more restrictive value is to be applied (in this case, the higher (!) age), that the formerly employed children receive a proper school education). In this regard, another example:

There are field workers in the United States who move from cropland to cropland to hire themselves out in order to earn family income.

Among these workers are, of course, families with children. In the United States, schooling is compulsory (the homeschooling option is not considered here).

Therefore, the children of the workers would have to be enrolled in school (or taken to kindergarten) in any new location where the parents find work.

In real life, this is not done. As a result, the children go to the fields with their parents to help them. Regardless of whether the children do this out of boredom, child labor is noted here.

7.3.2.3 Employment contracts

Only when those topmost checkpoints have been checked without any deviation, one can go back to the chart and the following sub-points will be dealt with:

1) With regard to service providers/subcontractors and employees, it is checked whether there is a complaint system in place.

As once declined above, a system must be behind once again in order that the processes/complaints can be traced.

What is the reason for this check?

Simply because employees of a service providers / subcontractors could file a complaint with you, e.g. that they feel forced to work without employment contracts.

2) Employment contracts:

Language of employment contracts:

$$Quota\ of\ Written\ Working\ Contracts = \frac{Number\ of\ Working\ Contracts\ (verbal + written)}{Number\ written\ Working\ Contracts}$$

Figure 26: Written Employment Contracts

$$Employment\ Contracts = \frac{Employment\ Contracts\ in\ (Local)Language}{Number\ Written\ Employment\ Contracts}$$

Figure 27 Written Employment Contracts (local language)

$$Working\ Contract = \frac{Working\ Contract\ in\ (Worker)\ Language}{Number\ written\ Working\ Contracts}$$

Figure 28 Written Employment Contracts (worker language)

So why is this important? Employees need to understand what they are signing!

Example: A new colleague with North Macedonian Nationality and language background is to work for a Swiss company.

Question 1: Which main language (German, French, Italian) is spoken in the Canton (Swiss Federal County)?

Question 2: Does the new colleague understand this language?

Question 3: If not, which language is used for communication?

Question 4: In which language is the employment contract? And, how can you ensure that the new colleague has understood:

a) What the contract states and b) what their duties are?

This leads to the obvious question:

Are all the mandatory elements available in the employment contract?

- legal components

- collective bargaining agreement components

After the examination of the employment contract basics, the wage and salary basics are still to be examined: Is there a legal minimum wage?

Is there a defined minimum living wage that must be complied with?

It can happen that the legal minimum wage is lower than the defined minimum living wage; in this case, the higher value is taken as a basis in favor of the employee.

This check is carried out explicitly within the remuneration section.

Likewise, prior to the actual remuneration check, it is checked whether a bonus system has been incorporated in the employment contract or its annexes.

A bonus system may never be constructed in such a way that the salary without the bonuses falls below the minimum living wage to be obtained.

If the bonuses are needed to reach the minimum (minimum wage or the defined minimum living wage), the aspect of forced labor must be examined, since the employees can only reach the minimum by working extra hours and, if applicable, overtime.

3) Verification of (historical) child labor.

The issue here is whether people were hired who, according to international standards, were younger than 15 years old when hired.

Although it may be permissible in some countries for persons as young as 14 to work, when in doubt, apply the international standards.

$$Employment\ Contracts\ (Age) \\ = (Employment\ Contracts\ Without\ Proof\ of\ Age) \\ /(Number\ of\ Written\ Employment\ Contracts)$$

Figure 29: Historical Child Labor

In the case of an actual audit, any child labor found must be responded to immediately; in the case of historical child labor, it must be investigated why this could have occurred.

For example, after World War II, the country of Belgium set the minimum age at 14 years because labor was needed for reconstruction.

7.3.2.4 Working hours

Following the assessment for child labor is a review of the working time regulations at hand. The ETI Base Code requires as Point 6:

6. Working hours are not excessive:

   6.1 Working hours must comply with national laws, collective agreements, and the provisions of 6.2 to 6.6 below, whichever affords the greater protection for workers. Sub-clauses 6.2 to 6.6 are based on international labor standards.

   6.2 Working hours, excluding overtime, shall be defined by contract, and shall not exceed 48 hours per week.*

   6.3 All overtime shall be voluntary. Overtime shall be used responsibly, taking into account all the following: the extent, frequency and hours worked by individual workers and the workforce as a whole. It shall not be used to replace regular employment. Overtime shall always be compensated at a premium rate, which is recommended to be not less than 125% of the regular rate of pay.

   6.4 The total hours worked in any seven-day period shall not exceed 60 hours, except where covered by clause 6.5 below.

   6.5 Working hours may exceed 60 hours in any seven-day period only in exceptional circumstances where all of the following are met:

   - This is allowed by national law;

   - This is allowed by a collective agreement freely negotiated with a workers' organization representing a significant portion of the workforce;

   - Appropriate safeguards are taken to protect the workers' health and safety; and

   - The employer can demonstrate that exceptional circumstances apply, such as unexpected production peaks, accidents or emergencies.

   6.6 Workers shall be provided with at least one day off in every seven day period or, where allowed by national law, two days off in every 14 day period.

To be examined are:

Are there legal regulations governing working hours, break times, rest periods, rest days and vacation days?

In general, the stricter requirement applies and is the basis for the audit.

This would mean that locally the valid regulation allows 80 hours of work per week, but the ETI Base Code in point 6.4 nor provides for a maximum of 60 hours.

In the audit, the more restrictive value (to the benefit of the employee) is always applied. Additional consideration must be given to whether local regulations regulate, for example, daily working hours.

Thus, daily and weekly working hours are verified in the audit. First verification value must therefore be:

$$(Maximum\ Permitted\ Working\ Time\ [Statutory\ or\ Collectively\ Agreed] \\ -\ Actual\ Working\ Time) \leq Maximum\ Permitted\ Working\ Time$$

Figure 30: Working Time

The following are then to be checked:

1) Rest breaks

Rest breaks are defined differently in each country!

Therefore, the legal and/or collective agreement requirements for rest breaks must be checked first.

$$(Actual\ Rest\ Break\ -\ Stipulated\ Rest\ Break\ [Statutory\ or\ Collectively\ Agreed]) \\ \geq\ Stipulated\ Rest\ Break$$

Figure 31: Rest Breaks

2) Rest days

Rest days are the days that are defined as days off in a period.

Here it is necessary to check whether the corresponding regulations have been complied with, and if not, whether there are any exceptions (which must then be complied with in an evident manner).

$$(Actual\ Rest\ Days\ -\ Stipulated\ Rest\ Days\ [Statutory\ or\ Collectively\ Agreed])$$
$$\geq Stipulated\ Rest\ Days$$

Figure 32: Rest Days

3) Vacation days

To regenerate and maintain performance, employees need rest periods, most of

$$(Actual\ Days\ of\ Leave\ -\ Stipulated\ Days\ of\ Leave\ [Statutory\ or\ Collectively\ Agreed])$$
$$\geq Stipulated\ Days\ of\ Leave$$

which are governed by law or, in some cases, by collective bargaining agreements.

Figure 33: Vacation days

7.3.3 Money

The following criteria have been added to the chart under "Money" (further criteria are possible):

	Code of Conduct	HSE	Contractor	Worker	Job	Money	HR	Managment System	Fire Safety & Accidents
		Key Indicators, Social Audits							
Managment System		Environment							
HR									
Money			Proper Payment				Payment Concept		
Job									
Worker									
Contractor									
HSE									
© Jens Schnuegger, 2023		Dormitory							

Figure 34: Important Checkpoints for Remuneration

The following requirements are postulated by the ETI Base Code:

5. Living wages are paid

   5.1 Wages and benefits paid for a standard working week meet, at a minimum, national legal standards or industry benchmark standards, whichever is higher. In any event, wages should always be enough to meet basic needs and to provide some discretionary income.

73

5.2 All workers shall be provided with written and understandable Information about their employment conditions with respect to wages before they enter employment and about the particulars of their wages for the pay period concerned each time that they are paid.

5.3 Deductions from wages as a disciplinary measure shall not be permitted, nor shall any deductions from wages not provided for by national law be permitted without the expressed permission of the worker concerned. All disciplinary measures should be recorded.

Applied to the individual facility, the following topics should be considered as minimum requirements:

7.3.3.1 Definition of the wage

Question: How are wages defined in your company?

What is intended here, is the way in which it is determined what wage is paid.

Definitions are predominantly:

a) Collectively agreed wages or

b) Individual wage setting.

Therefore, the first step to check is: Is there a valid, applicable collective bargaining agreement. If so, then the following applies:

$$(Wage\ According\ to\ Payroll\ -\ Wage\ According\ to\ Collective\ Bargaining\ Agreement\ ) \geq 0$$

Figure 35: Checking Collectively Agreed Wages

The value "zero" stands for the parity of the found wage and the collectively agreed wage. If the value found is less than 0, the collectively agreed wage is being violated (underpaid).

In addition, it is necessary to check whether the collective bargaining agreement is correctly applied. It may happen that the value of the wage corresponds to the collective bargaining agreement, but the employee is incorrectly classified. In this case, the remuneration would again fall short of the collective agreement wage. The check is somewhat more extensive in the case of individual wages, as various scenarios must be considered with this constellation.

Since no collective bargaining agreement is applicable, it is necessary to perform separate test loops:

1) Does the company adhere to the collective bargaining agreement? This means that the company is not bound by a collective bargaining agreement, but nevertheless uses the collective bargaining agreement as a basis for remuneration. In this case, the wage check is again performed against the valid collective bargaining agreement.

2) The company takes the collective bargaining agreement as a benchmark. In this case, the wages are usually below the collective agreement wage, but the collective agreement increases are nevertheless implemented.

3) The company has its own wage structure, apart from the collective bargaining agreement, and only this is to be applied.

$$(Wage\ According\ to\ Payroll\ -\ Minimum\ Wage\ (or\ Living\ Wage)\,) \geq 0$$

Figure 36: Minimum wage check

In this case, too, the minimum wage is not attained if the value is below 0.

7.3.3.2 Implementation in the Facility

Irrespective of the test for compliance with the minimum wage that has just been undertaken, further test routines are necessary.

1. Examination of work areas

Are all workplaces valued equally?

It is necessary to check whether all employees, who perform the same activities, are paid the same wages. If differences are noted, an explanation must be given as to how they occur and what the reason is behind these differences.

Are all of the positions filled with the corresponding qualifications?

This is particularly about whether it is possible to fill selective positions with temporary workers and why this is the situation.

Example: Temporary workers are used for hazardous work in order to protect the company's own workforce.

2. Examination of workforce deployment

This is where it is necessary to check whether all employees are paid the same wages for performing the same tasks. This check refers to the wages of women and men and also from local to foreign colleagues.

Reference is made here to the work on site in the audited company.

Thus, at this point, the proof is to be provided that equal remuneration is paid.

This check is again made against the compensation aspect, but in addition also against the discrimination aspect. The ETI Base Code states:

7. No discrimination is practiced.

7.1 There is no discrimination in hiring, compensation, access to training, promotion, termination or retirement based on race, caste, national origin, religion, age, disability, gender, marital status, sexual orientation, union membership or political affiliation.

The relevant checkpoints are consequently:

$$Knowledge\ Person\ 1 = Knowledge\ Person\ 2$$

$$(Remuneration\ Person\ 1 - Remuneration\ Person\ 2\ [\neq Person\ 1]) = 0$$

Figure 37: Equal Treatment Job

This implies that person 2 has different characteristics than person 1. This may result in a possible discrimination aspect.

To illustrate: Person 1 is a trained technician from Country A, Person 2 is a trained technician from Country C, who is now working in Country A.

It is checked whether both receive the same salary ("seniority" discounted).

7.3.3.3 External Applicability

Your company uses its own code of conduct, or has been requested by a customer to use at least theirs.

This code of conduct indicates an obligation to apply the social standards in your supply chain accordingly.

As an example, you are using contract workers.

To ensure complete evacuation in the event of a fire, the contract workers use the internal clocking system.

At the same time, the contract labor company generates its invoice to your company based on these hourly records.

Therefore, you can easily check if the company is billing you for the correct number of hours.

What you cannot see is whether the contracting company is paying its employees correctly. You are responsible for this check, dictated by the Code of Conduct.

For example: During an audit of a company, the time sheets of the welders were presented. Surprisingly, some of the timesheets had been created mechanically (Excel) and some manually. In the case of the manual lists, all entries were made with the same handwriting and, in addition, all employees started at 08:00, went to break at the same time and stopped punctually at 16:30.

Beforehand, in the employee interviews, the employees presented their own timesheets, so that before the examination in the HR department, it had long been known what hours were actually worked.

It turns out that, according to the data provided, the employees had worked 40 hours per week. The individual records showed 65 hours worked.

The company was billed for 65 hours per week.

This resulted in a difference of 25 hours that were missing from the employee's payroll. After this was noted, the challenge in the audit was to find out what had happened to the remaining unbilled hours, especially since the employees had stated in the interview that they would be paid on time for all hours worked (plus a bonus for overtime). It was discovered that the bonus resulted from the fact that the supposedly missing hours were paid directly (without deductions).

To avoid these structures, contract workers and employees of service providers are always in the scope (i.e., the scope of the applied audit catalog) of the audit, and it is the responsibility of the audited company to obtain and provide the data requested in the audit.

If this data cannot be provided, it must be assumed in the case of doubt that there are forced labor structures to the disadvantage of the audited company.

7.3.4 Occupational Health and Safety (OH&S)

The model in the illustration focuses on the management of Occupational Health and Safety, the handling of waste and the handling of, possibly, accidents. In this case, too, the list is not conclusive.

Foundations of Workplace Safety Organization (workplace-related) e.g. safety equipment or machine safety.

- How is Occupational Health and Safety organized?

- Who is the responsible person?

- If the task has been delegated, how are the competencies regulated?

The requirements according to the ETI Base Code are: Working conditions are safe and hygienic.

	Key Indicators, Social Audits						
	HSE	Contractor	Worker	Job	Money	HR	Managment System
Managment System	Environment						
HR							
Money							
Job							
Worker							
Contractor							
HSE				Waste Handling			
		HSE Committee				Accidents	
© Jens Schnuegger, 2023	Dormitory						

Figure 38: Important checkpoints for Occupational Health and Safety

3.1 A safe and hygienic working environment shall be provided, bearing in mind the prevailing knowledge of the industry and of any specific hazards. Adequate steps shall be taken to prevent accidents and injury to health arising out of, associated with, or occurring in the course of work, by minimizing, so far as is reasonably practicable, the causes of hazards inherent in the working environment.

3.2 Workers shall receive regular and recorded health and safety training, and such training shall be repeated for new or reassigned workers.

3.3 Access to clean toilet facilities and to potable water, and, if appropriate, sanitary facilities for food storage shall be provided.

3.4 Accommodation, where provided, shall be clean, safe, and meet the basic needs of the workers.

3.5 The company observing the code shall assign responsibility for health and safety to a senior management representative.

These requirements must be met.

7.3.4.1 Systematic Occupational Health and Safety

Do you have an occupational safety concept and is it organized?

In ISO 9001 and ISO 45001, the question would be, "How do you ensure that a consistent occupational safety system is followed in the company and that employees know who is responsible in each case?

Written safety concept? Yes/No → If no: Set up!

Are all legal bases known and how do you ensure that all documents and references are up-to-date?

Legal register: Yes/No → If No: Set up!

If you answer these two questions with: "Yes, but external", then please additionally check whether the external responsible person uses current data. The responsibility, here in the inspection, is with you! It is your task to ensure on site that all data is up to date!

7.3.4.2 Operational safety

Companies should find operational safety a simple area to verify, as they should have existing internal safety structures in place.

The simplest example of non-compliance: Open oil cans stored between fan heater and packaging material. A fire extinguisher was not in the immediate area.(Note: found in Western Europe).

All of the questions listed below are just the tip of the iceberg, and it should be assumed that every company asks itself these questions.

It is obvious that hazards to employees and/or the environment are unacceptable.

7.3.4.4 Machine safety

- What are the organizational criteria for machine safety?
- Can employees injure themselves on the machine in the course of performing work steps?
- Have the co-workers been verifiably trained on the machines?
- Do the machine users feel that their workplace meets the requirements?
- How often are machines maintained? And is this documented?
- Many other points can be questioned in the audit; it will then be decisive that you have preventively questioned as many as possible (or know where you can find the questioned data).

81

7.3.4.4 Electrical safety

- Are all cable connections properly secured?

- At what intervals are cable connections checked?

- At what intervals are major equipment and/or electrical cabinets tested?

- Are electrical hand tools safe to use?

- Are cable connections properly attached? (Or can so-called "monkey swings" be found?

- Is there an inventory of electrical equipment?

- ... and, and

7.3.4.5 Workplace safety

- Is the working environment for each employee safe?

- Are floors slippery?

- Is special personal protective equipment needed?

- Is this protective equipment used?

- ... and, and

7.3.4.6 Institutional Occupational Health and Safety

- Is there an occupational safety committee?

- How often does the health and safety committee meet? - Are meetings documented in minutes?

- Are findings followed up? - Is there a responsible manager who is authorized to make decisions when occupational safety measures are necessary?

- ... the list can be extended here as well.

7.3.4.7 Waste Management

- What types of waste are generated?

- Is there any hazardous waste?

- Which employees are responsible for waste disposal?

- Are colleagues sufficiently and demonstrably trained?

- Where is waste (temporarily) stored on the site?

- How is the waste disposed of?

- Who is responsible for disposal? Internally/externally?

- Can quantities be controlled and tracked?

- ... the list can be extended here as well.

7.3.5 Workplace (Job)

		HSE	Contractor	Worker	Job	Money	HR	Managment System	
Managment System		Environment							
HR									
Money									
Job	Code of Conduct	Machine Syfety			Job Promotion		Job Description		Fire Safety & Accidents
		Overtime			Job Cluster				
		E-Safety							
		Working Hours							
		Workspace Safety			Gender Dependent				
		Rest Breaks							
Worker									
Contractor									
HSE									
® Jens Schnuegger, 2023		Dormitory							

Key Indicators, Social Audits

Figure 39: Important check points on the subject of the workplace

83

The subject area workplace comprises various aspects.

In the graphic, various checkpoints are again listed as examples.

First of all, the cross-checking of the points listed in the "Occupational Health and Safety" section applies here.

It is important to point out once again that a social/ethical audit always focuses on the employee. Even if the Occupational Health and Safety audit did not reveal any deviations, this is repeated here under the aspect of "employee hazards" and checked from a different angle.

At this point, if not earlier, one realizes that these audits have a different approach and that a nice employee handbook is only one thing: "nice".

If the implementation is not done, or only rudimentarily, this is conspicuous no later than at this point.

In addition, the specifications from the HR department are scrutinized under this checkpoint: working hours, overtime, remuneration (normal hours and overtime), rest periods, breaks, vacation, special payments, etc.

These cross-references and cross-checks are followed by an in-depth examination of the workplace organization.

Checkpoint can be e.g. whether the employee is qualified to do the job or not:

$$Job\ Performed = \frac{Qualification + Training}{Job\ Description}$$

Figure 40: Job qualification

The first thing to check is whether the right employee is assigned to the right job. This is followed by an examination according to the discrimination rules, e.g.

- Can any person apply for this particular job?
- Are there any restrictions based on gender, creed, nationality, or something similar?

Back to the workplace: - Is there an opportunity to check dependencies?

- Is there a job description?
- Is there a training plan that covers employee development?
- Is the job description known to the employee?
- Are areas of responsibility and authority defined?
- Is the supervisor structure known? Which supervisor is the contact person for which question?
- Have the employees been instructed in this?
  With the production process it can be reviewed:
- Is there a material requirements plan?
- What materials must be available at the workplace?
- How are replenishments organized?
- Is there a reporting system for material defects?
- Is there a quality control system?

Why do you have to look here? - There is the possibility that employees have to pay for materials.

- Do employees have to pay for corrective actions out of their own pocket?

- Are there warnings for errors or error frequency?

- Are the warnings monetary? (Is money deducted for errors)?

The situation in each individual company is all-important at this point.

- How is the individual company set up?

- What does the auditor see during the tour of the company?

- How does the auditor perceive individual situations?

The questions that the auditor asks in the company are always related to the situation found.

There is no 100% preparation, if something looks too good, it will also be questioned. Potemkin villages[62] are recognized and branded as such.

Please keep in mind that these inspections are not meant to hassle a company or even an entrepreneur.

The purpose of these questions is to protect the most valuable resource, the human being, from exploitation and abuse.

---

62 Prince Grigory Alexandrovich Potemkin (also: Potyomkin) was responsible for the population of the Black Sea region by peasants and citizens under Catherine the Great. During a trip through the Crimea, the tsarina took a look at Potemkin's work. Meanwhile, rumors were spreading in St. Petersburg - presumably by people who were angry at not being allowed to take part in the trip - that Potemkin had merely set up villages of painted house facades to impress the tsarina with his successes. Due to the works of the Saxon envoy in St. Petersburg, which were considered serious, the mere slander was long believed to be the truth.
https://de.wiktionary.org/wiki/Potemkinsches_Dorf (Retrieved: 03.OCT.2023)

7.3.6 Employee / Worker

		HSE	Contractor	Worker	Job	Money	HR	Managment System	
Key Indicators, Social Audits									
Managment System	Code of Conduct	Environment							Fire Safety & Accidents
HR									
Money									
Job									
Worker			Workers Committee				Contact Possibility		
			Union					Recruitment Abroad	
Contractor									
HSE									
© Jens Schnuegger, 2023		Dormitory							

Figure 41: Important checkpoints on the workforce

The approaches to the criteria from the graphic are similar to those already discussed in the personnel section, but they are now supplemented by the complex of freedom of association. This does not necessarily mean that the questions have the same intention as the previous ones, but rather that the criteria are examined from the perspective of the employees. If the questioning is done from the perspective of the employees, then you will note that the question complexes are kind of redundant.

Approaches under consideration may include the following examples:

1. Different tasks for salaried workers and/or temporary workers, and if so, why?

   - Domestic vs. foreign workers.

   - Are employees recruited abroad?

2. Is there an organigram?

3. - How are responsibilities organized?

4 Are all contact persons known?

5 Is there a complaint system?

   - What channels are available?

   - How are complaints managed?

6 Freedom of Association, etc.

7 Is there a bonus system?

8 Is overtime voluntary?

9 How many hours are the standard working hours?

10 How are breaks organized?

11 Is there employee representation? And in what form?

12 Is there a trade union?

13 Are the persons discriminated or hindered in any way?

14 Did the employees have to make any payments to be able to work for you?

   - Direct payment to the company?

   - Payment to a placement agency?

   - Travel and visa expenses?

15 Is there an occupational safety committee that is responsible, with decision-making authority, for workplace safety in the company?

7.3.7 Subcontractor (Service Provider)

	Key Indicators, Social Audits							
		HSE	Contractor	Worker	Job	Money	HR	Managment System	
Managment System	Code of Conduct	Environment							Fire Safety & Accidents
HR									
Money									
Job									
Worker									
Contractor			Sub-Contracting	Recruitment Fee			Written Contract	Recruitment Abroad	
				Debt Scheme			Proper Contract details		
			Out-scourcing				Contract Language		
HSE									
© Jens Schnuegger, 2023		Dormitory							

42: Important check topics regarding External Companies

The subject of subcontractors is not currently audited in depth by all companies. Just as you are audited by your customer, you are required to audit your supply chain.

It is important to distinguish between:

- Subcontractors (working in the process) and
- Service providers (e.g. temporary employment agencies, cleaning, security, catering).

First, group and rank the companies:

1. What subcontractors are working on the site?

2. In which areas of operation are these companies active?

3. Additive or substitutive activities?

4. Who are the internal contact(s)?

Hereafter, the same check loops will be run through, which also apply to your internal employees.

1. Different tasks for salaried workers and/or temporary workers, and if so, why?

   - Domestic vs. foreign workers.

   - Are employees recruited abroad?

2. Is there an organigram?

3. How are responsibilities organized?

4. Are all contact persons known?

5. Is there a complaint system?

   - What channels are available?

   - How are complaints managed?

6. Freedom of Association, etc.

7. Is there a bonus system?

8. Is overtime voluntary?

9. How many hours are the standard working hours?

10. How are breaks organized?

11. Is there employee representation? And in what form?

12. Is there a trade union?

13. Are the persons discriminated or hindered in any way?

14. Did the employees have to make any payments to be able to work for you?

    - Direct payment to the company?

    - Payment to a placement agency?

    - Travel and visa expenses?

15. Is there an occupational safety committee that is responsible, with decision-making authority, for workplace safety in the company?

Ask yourself the question:

"Is it sufficient to receive a paper from your supplier confirming that all compliance requirements are met, or is it better to verify it on site?"

As a rule, the more remote a supplier is, the less you know about the circumstances on the ground.

However, this is what this audit is all about, the working conditions of workers in the supply chain.

8

Preparation

To prepare properly for a social audit, it is important to understand what is to be achieved through supply chain legislation. Using Germany as an example, it can be noted that two different ministries deal with supply chain legislation: On the one hand, the Federal Ministry of Labor and Social Affairs (acts internally) and on the other hand, the Federal Ministry for Economic Cooperation and Development (works externally).

Just as two federal ministries deal with the various sub-aspects of the law, it is expected that each company will also deal with these aspects.

The internal perspective is easier for the vast majority of companies, as these aspects are usually part of their daily work routine. More challenging, as currently hardly common practice, is the external perspective, which includes suppliers, subcontractors and service providers.

This book aims to provide an approach on how to prepare in a structured way and what supply chain legislation aims to achieve.

The previous chapters have been guided by the ETI Base Code and have given you an overview on what the requirements and intentions of this code are.

Even though the ETI Base Code has been chosen as a basis, the preparation for a social audit according to the ICS standard is comparable.

In the appendix, both standards are included as a repository of information, with the status at the time the book went to press.

An audit against the ETI Base Code or the ICS Standard takes varying amounts of time, as the duration is staggered by company size.

Depending on customer or client specifications, exams are announced with specific dates or, semi-announced, within a time frame.

For you: Prepare for your audit by creating a list of possible documents and establishing access logic. Be guided by the exam topics provided by the two codes:

I.   Management System

II. discrimination

III. freedom of association, collective bargaining

IV. Working Conditions

    i.   Minimum age, child labor

    ii. Forced labor

    iii. Minimum wage

    iv. Social benefits

    v. Working hours

    vi. Disciplinary action, harassment, abuse

V. Work Environment

    i. Safe working conditions, hygiene

    ii.   Accident prevention

    iii. Medical care

    iv. Training and instruction

The availability of documents ensures that one can concentrate on individual topics in the audit and thus avoid jumping around in the topics. The audit process can thus be approached in a structured manner.

9

THE ETI BASE CODE

9.1   Employment is freely chosen

1.1. There is no forced, bonded or involuntary prison labour.

1.2.   Workers are not required to lodge "deposits" or their identity papers with their employer and are free to leave their employer after reasonable notice.

9.2 Freedom of association and the right to collective bargaining are respected

2.1 Workers, without distinction, have the right to join or form trade unions of their own choosing and to bargain collectively.

2.2 The employer adopts an open attitude towards the activities of trade unions and their organisational activities.

2.3 Workers' representatives are not discriminated against and have access to carry out their representative functions in the workplace.

2.4 Where the right to freedom of association and collective bargaining is restricted under law, the employer facilitates, and does not hinder the development of parallel means for independent and free association and bargaining.

9.3 Working conditions are safe and hygienic

3.1 A safe and hygienic working environment shall be provided, bearing in mind the prevailing knowledge of the industry and of any specific hazards. Adequate steps shall be taken to prevent accidents and injury to health arising out of, associated with, or occurring in the course of work, by minimising, so far as is reasonably practicable, the causes of hazards inherent in the working environment.

3.2 Workers shall receive regular and recorded health and safety training, and such training shall be repeated for new or reassigned workers.

3.3 Access to clean toilet facilities and to potable water, and, if appropriate, sanitary facilities for food storage shall be provided.

3.4 Accommodation, where provided, shall be clean, safe, and meet the basic needs of the workers.

3.5 The company observing the code shall assign responsibility for health and safety to a senior management representative.

9.4 Child labor shall not be used

4.1 There shall be no new recruitment of child labor.

4.2 Companies shall develop or participate in and contribute to policies and programmes which provide for the transition of any child found to be performing child labor to enable her or him to attend and remain in quality education until no longer a child; "child" and "child labor" being defined in the appendices.

4.3 Children and young persons under 18 shall not be employed at night or in hazardous conditions.

4.4 These policies and procedures shall conform to the provisions of the relevant ILO standards.

9.5 Living wages are paid

5.1 Wages and benefits paid for a standard working week meet, at a minimum, national legal standards or industry benchmark standards, whichever is higher. In any event wages should always be enough to meet basic needs and to provide some discretionary income.

5.2 All workers shall be provided with written and understandable Information about their employment conditions in respect to wages before they enter employment and about the particulars of their wages for the pay period concerned each time that they are paid.

5.3 Deductions from wages as a disciplinary measure shall not be permitted nor shall any deductions from wages not provided for by national law be permitted without the expressed permission of the worker concerned. All disciplinary measures should be recorded.

9.6 Working hours are not excessive

6.1 Working hours must comply with national laws, collective agreements, and the provisions of 6.2 to 6.6 below, whichever affords greater protection for workers. Sub-clauses 6.2 to 6.6 are based on international labor standards.

6.2 Working hours, excluding overtime, shall be defined by contract, and shall not exceed 48 hours per week. [International standards recommend the progressive reduction of normal hours of work, when appropriate, to 40 hours per week, without any reduction in workers' wages as hours are reduced.]

6.3 All overtime shall be voluntary. Overtime shall be used responsibly, taking into account all the following: the extent, frequency and hours worked by individual workers and the workforce as a whole. It shall not be used to replace regular employment. Overtime shall always be compensated at a premium rate, which is recommended to be not less than 125% of the regular rate of pay.

6.4 The total hours worked in any seven-day period shall not exceed 60 hours, except where covered by clause 6.5 below.

6.5 Working hours may exceed 60 hours in any seven-day period only in exceptional circumstances where all of the following are met:

- This is allowed by national law;

- This is allowed by a collective agreement freely negotiated with a workers' organisation representing a significant portion of the workforce;

- Appropriate safeguards are taken to protect the workers' health and safety; and

- The employer can demonstrate that exceptional circumstances apply such as unexpected production peaks, accidents or emergencies.

6.6 Workers shall be provided with at least one day off in every seven-day period or, where allowed by national law, two days off in every 14-day period.

9.7 No discrimination is practiced

7.1 There is no discrimination in hiring, compensation, access to training, promotion, termination or retirement based on race, caste, national origin, religion, age, disability, gender, marital status, sexual orientation, union membership or political affiliation.

9.8 Regular employment is provided

8.1 To every extent possible, work performed must be on the basis of recognised employment relationship established through national law and practice.

8.2 Obligations to employees under labour or social security laws and regulations arising from the regular employment relationship shall not be avoided through the use of labour-only contracting, sub-contracting, or homeworking arrangements, or through apprenticeship schemes where there is no real intent to impart skills or provide regular employment, nor shall any such obligations be avoided through the excessive use of fixed-term contracts of employment.

9.9 No harsh or inhumane treatment is allowed

9.1 Physical abuse or discipline, the threat of physical abuse, sexual or other harassment and verbal abuse or other forms of intimidation shall be prohibited.

10

ICS Social Code of Conduct

10.1 Management system, transparency and traceability

1. The supplier shall put in place an efficient internal management system to ensure that:

a. all employment relationships are acknowledged and documented (in accordance with national laws, customs and practices and international employment standards) from the time of recruitment until the end of the employment contract; particularly in the case of employees with a special status: young employees, immigrants, national migrants, seasonal workers, homeworkers, piece workers, interns or apprentices, contract workers, temporary workers, etc.;

b. all the company's sales and management activities are carried out transparently and correctly recorded in the company's registers;

c. the principles set forth in this Code are circulated and applied consistently within the supplier's organization;

d. the supplier shall detect all acts which breach the principles of this Code, determine the underlying causes of problems identified and implement measures to deal with such acts effectively in accordance with national laws, customs and practices and international employment standards;

e. the persons in charge of applying this Code and more generally the associated legal aspects concerning employment law, security and the environment are informed and trained;

f. action is taken against all forms of corruption, extortion, embezzlement and bribery;

g. its impact on the surrounding community, natural resources and the environment in general is analyzed so that the necessary procedures can be put in place to prevent and minimize the negative effects connected with the partner's operations;

2. The supplier undertakes to circulate the principles of this Code to its entire supply and sub-contracting chain:

a. The supplier shall disclose to the ICS client, before any order is placed by the client, a list of the factories belonging to the supplier and its sub-contractors (companies authorized by the supplier to handle all or part of the final production supposed to be produced by the supplier). ICS clients do not permit their orders to be produced in a factory which does not comply with this Code. Once the ICS client has confirmed an order, the supplier is not authorized to change the previously disclosed list of factories or sub-contractors. If it is necessary for any reason to change the list of supplier and sub-contractor factories, a written agreement shall be obtained from the ICS client.

b. The supplier shall check that the factories or sub-contractors identified in the ICS client's production chain comply with the principles of this Code.

c. If the supplier becomes aware of breaches of the principles of this Code in its supply and sub-contracting chain, it shall immediately inform the ICS client and shall undertake to implement a corrective action plan for the supplier/sub-contractor concerned. If the supplier/sub-contractor refuses to cooperate, the supplier shall undertake to terminate its collaboration with the supplier/sub-contractor concerned.

10.2 Minimum Age, Child Labor and Young Workers

1. The supplier shall comply with the national minimum age for admission to employment or work in any occupation, which should not be less than the age for completing compulsory schooling and, in any case, not be inferior to 15 years old. If however, the local legal minimum age is set at 14 years of age in accordance with ILO Convention 138 developing country exceptions, this lower age may apply.

2. The supplier shall neither recruit nor exploit children in any way. If children are found on the production site, (except in a childcare room), the supplier shall seek a sensitive and satisfactory solution that puts the best interests of the child first.

3. The supplier shall not employ young workers under the age of 18 years old at night, or in conditions which could jeopardize their health, their safety or their moral integrity, and/or which could harm their physical, mental, spiritual, moral or social development in accordance with ILO Convention 182.

10.3 Forced labor

1. All work must be conducted on a voluntary basis, and not under threat of any penalty or sanctions.

2. The use of forced or compulsory or unpaid labor in all its forms, including prison labor when not in accordance with Convention 29, and unpaid overtime work, is prohibited.

3. The supplier shall not require workers to make unreasonable deposits/financial guarantees and shall not confiscate identity documents off any worker (such as passports, identity cards, etc.). No abusive delayed payment of wages shall occur.

4. Bonded labor is prohibited. The supplier shall not use any form of bonded labor nor permit or encourage workers to incur debt through recruitment fees or other means.

5. Indentured labor is prohibited. The supplier shall respect the right of workers to terminate their employment after legal notice. The supplier shall respect the right of workers to leave the workplace and factory after their shift.

10.4 Non-Discrimination

1. The supplier shall respect equal opportunities in terms of recruitment, compensation, access to training, promotion, termination or retirement.

2. The supplier shall not engage in, support or tolerate discrimination in employment including recruitment, hiring, training, working conditions, job assignments, pay, benefits, promotions, discipline, termination or retirement on the basis of gender, age, religion, marital status, race, caste, social background, diseases, disability, pregnancy, ethnic and national origin, nationality, membership in worker organizations including unions, political affiliation, sexual orientation, or any other personal characteristics.

3. The supplier shall base all terms and conditions of employment on an individual's ability to do the job, not on the basis of personal characteristics or beliefs.

10.5 Disciplinary practices, harassment and abuse

1. The supplier shall treat all workers with respect and dignity.

2. The supplier shall not engage in or tolerate bullying, harassment or abuse of any kind.

3. The supplier shall establish written disciplinary procedures and shall explain them in clear and understandable terms to their workers. All disciplinary actions shall be recorded.

10.6 Freedom of association and grievance mechanisms

1. Workers have the right to join or form trade unions of their own choosing and to bargain collectively, without prior authorization from supplier's management. The supplier shall not interfere with, obstruct or prevent such legitimate activities.

2. Where the right to freedom of association and collective bargaining is restricted or prohibited under law, the supplier shall not hinder alternative forms of independent and free workers representation and negotiation, in accordance with ILO conventions.

3. The supplier shall not discriminate against or otherwise penalize worker representatives or trade union members because of their membership in or affiliation with a trade union, or their legitimate trade union activity in accordance with ILO conventions.

4. The supplier shall give internal worker representatives access to the workplace in order to carry out their representative functions in accordance with ILO conventions.

5. The supplier shall make all possible efforts to maintain or participate in an effective information feedback and grievance mechanism at the operational level to be able to respond to individuals and communities.

10.7 Working hours and overtime

1. The supplier shall set working hours that comply with national laws and ILO conventions, whichever affords greater protection to ensure the health, safety and welfare of workers.

2. The supplier shall respect that the standard allowable working hours in a week are 48, excluding overtime. Workers shall not be required to work in excess of 48 hours per week on a regular basis.

3. Overtime shall be voluntary and shall not exceed 8 (eight) hours per week and shall not be requested on a regular basis.

4. The supplier shall respect all workers' right to at least one rest day in every 7 (seven) day period as well as annual paid leave period and public national and local holidays as per local regulations.

10.8 Remuneration and benefits

1. The supplier must compensate its workers by providing wages, overtime pay, benefits and paid leave, which respectively meet or exceed legal minimum and/or industry benchmark standards and/or collective agreements, whichever is higher.

2. Acknowledging the fundamental nature of remuneration for workers and those who are dependent on them, ICS expects that the supplier shall not consider the legal minimum wage as an end in itself, but as a mere threshold not to be reached but to be exceeded, the goal sought to be that this remuneration should be able to cover basic needs whilst guaranteeing a discretionary income.

3. The supplier shall always compensate all workers for all overtime at a premium rate, as required by law and, where applicable, by contractual agreement.

4. The supplier shall provide all legally required benefits, including paid leave, to all workers.

5. The supplier shall not make any deductions from wages which are unauthorized or not provided for by national law. The supplier shall not make any deduction from wages as a disciplinary measure.

6. The supplier shall provide all workers with written and understandable information about their employment conditions, including wages, before they

enter into employment; and about details of their wages for the pay period concerned each time they are paid.

7. Work performed must be on the basis of a recognized employment relationship established in compliance with national legislation and ILO conventions, whichever affords the greater protection.

8. Labor-only contracting, sub-contracting or homeworking arrangements, apprenticeship schemes where there is no real intent to impart skills or provide regular employment, excessive use of fixed term contracts of employment, or any comparable arrangements shall not be used to avoid obligations to workers under labor or social security laws and regulations arising from the regular employment relationship.

10.9 Health and safety

Provisions under Health and safety shall be further defined to cater for specific conditions and related hazards pertaining to different industries, in accordance with the relevant applicable Health & Safety principles:

1. The supplier shall provide safe and clean conditions in all work and residential facilities and shall establish and follow a clear set of procedures regulating occupational health and safety.

2. The supplier must take adequate steps to prevent accidents and injury to health arising out of, associated with, or occurring in the course of work, by minimizing, so far as is reasonably practicable, the causes of hazards inherent in the working environment. Appropriate and effective personal protective equipment shall be provided as needed.

3. The supplier shall provide access to adequate medical assistance and facilities.

4. The supplier shall provide all workers with access to clean toilet facilities and to drinkable water and, if applicable, sanitary facilities for food preparation and storage.

5. The supplier shall ensure that residential facilities for workers, where provided, are clean and safe.

6. The supplier shall assign the responsibility for health and safety to a senior management representative.

7. The supplier shall provide regular and recorded health and safety training to workers and management, and such training shall be repeated for all new or reassigned workers and management.

8. The supplier shall provide adequate safeguards against fire, and shall ensure the strength, stability and safety of buildings and equipment, including residential facilities where provided.

9. The supplier shall undertake sufficient training of workers and management in waste management, handling and disposal of chemicals and other dangerous materials.

10.10 The supplier is required to comply with

1. OECD Guidelines for Multinational Enterprises, 2011.

2. UN Guiding principles on business and human rights, 2011

3. International conventions on fundamental human rights:

   -The International Covenant on Civil and Political Rights, 1966

   -The International Covenant on Economic, Social and Cultural Rights, 1966

   -The Convention on the Elimination of All Forms of Discrimination against Women, 1980

   -The Convention on the Rights of the Child, 1990

   -The Convention on the Rights of Persons with Disabilities, 2007

4. Fundamental international labor standards as defined by the ILO Declaration on Fundamental Principles and Rights at Work and its Follow-up:

    -C87, Freedom of Association and Protection of the Right to Organize Convention, 1948

    -C98, Right to Organize and Collective Bargaining Convention, 1949

    -C29, Forced Labor Convention, 1930

    -C105, Abolition of Forced Labor Convention, 1957

    -C138, Minimum Age Convention, 1973

    -C182, Worst Forms of Child Labor Convention, 1999

    -C100, Equal Remuneration Convention, 1951

    -C111, Discrimination (Employment and Occupation) Convention, 1958

5. Other applicable international labor standards, such as:

    -The ILO call for Decent Work

    -C1, Hours of Work (Industry) Convention, 1919

    -C14, Weekly Rest (Industry) Convention, 1921

    -C95, Protection of Wages Convention, 1949

    -C131, Minimum Wage Fixing Convention, 1970

    -C135, Workers' Representatives Convention, 1971

    -C155, Occupational Safety and Health Convention, 1981

    -C161, Occupational Health Services Convention, 1985

    -R85, Protection of Wages Recommendation, 1949

    -R116, Reduction of Hours of Work Recommendation, 1962

    -R135, Minimum Wage Fixing Recommendation, 1970

    -R164, Occupational Safety and Health Recommendation, 1981

    -R184, Home Work Recommendation, 1996

    -R190, Worst Forms of Child Labor Convention Recommendation, 1999

6. Applicable national and/ or local legislation.

    - The provisions of this Code constitute minimum and not maximum standards.

    - This Code shall not be used to prevent international labor standards or national and/or local legislations from being exceeded.

11

[German] Act on Corporate Due Diligence in Supply Chains

Not approved translation/information purpose only

Resources: https://www.gesetze-im-internet.de/lksg/ or PDF in english https://www.csr-in-deutschland.de/SharedDocs/Downloads/EN/act-corporate-due -diligence-obligations-supply-chains.pdf?_blob=publicationFile&v=3

Extract from the Law on Corporate Due Diligence to Prevent Human Rights Violations in Supply Chains (Supply Chain Due Diligence Act - LkSG).

11.1 § 1 Scope of Application

(1) This Act shall apply to enterprises, irrespective of their legal form, which.

1. Have their head office, principal place of business, administrative headquarters or registered office in Germany, and

2. Generally employ at least 3,000 employees in Germany; employees posted abroad are included.

Notwithstanding sentence 1 number 1, this Act shall also apply to enterprises, irrespective of their legal form, which

3. Have a branch office in Germany pursuant to Section 13d of the German Commercial Code, and

4. Generally employ at least 3,000 employees in Germany.

As of January 1, 2024, the thresholds provided for in sentence 1 number 2 and sentence 2 number 2 shall each be 1,000 employees.

(2) Temporary workers shall be included in the calculation of the number of employees (subsection 1, sentence 1, number 2 and sentence 2, number 2) of the user enterprise if the period of employment exceeds six months.

(3) Within affiliated companies (Section 15 of the German Stock Corporation Act), the employees employed in Germany by all companies belonging to the group shall be included in the calculation of the number of employees (subsection 1, sentence 1, number 2) of the parent company; employees posted abroad shall be included.

11.2 § 3 Duty of Care

(1) Businesses shall be required to exercise due diligence in their supply chains in accordance with the human rights and environmental due diligence requirements set out in this section, with the aim of preventing or minimizing human rights or environmental risks or ending the violation of human rights or environmental obligations. Due diligence obligations include:

1. The establishment of a risk management system (Section 4 (1)),

2. The establishment of an in-house responsibility (Section 4(3)),

3. The performance of regular risk analyses (§ 5),

4. The issuance of a policy statement (§ 6 Paragraph 2),

5. The establishment of preventive measures in the company's own business area

   (§ 6 Paragraphs 1 and 3) and vis-à-vis direct suppliers (§ 6 Paragraph 4),

6. The taking of corrective measures (§ 7 Paragraphs 1 to 3),

7. The establishment of a complaints procedure (§ 8),

8. The implementation of due diligence with respect to risks at indirect suppliers (§ 9), and

9. The documentation (Section 10 (1)) and reporting (Section 10 (2)).

(2) The appropriate manner of acting in compliance with the due diligence obligations shall be determined according to:

1. The nature and scope of the company's business activities,

2. The company's ability to influence the direct perpetrator of a human rights or environment-related risk or the violation of a human rights-related or environment-related duty,

3. The typically expected severity of the violation, the reversibility of the violation, and the likelihood of the violation of a human rights-related or an environment-related obligation, as well as

4. The nature of the company's causal contribution to the human rights or environment-related risk or to the violation of human rights or

5. Environment-related duty.

(3) A breach of the obligations under this Act shall not give rise to civil liability. Civil liability established independently of this Act shall remain unaffected.

11.3 § 4 Risk Management

(1) Companies shall establish an appropriate and effective risk management system to ensure compliance with due diligence obligations (Section 3 (1)). Risk management shall be embedded in all relevant business processes through appropriate measures.

(2) Effective measures are those that enable the identification and minimization of human rights and environmental risks and the prevention, cessation or minimization of the extent of violations of human rights or environmental obligations where the enterprise has caused or contributed to such risks or violations within the supply chain.

(3) The company shall ensure that it is determined who within the company is responsible for overseeing risk management, such as through the appointment of a human rights officer. The management shall obtain information on the work of the responsible person or persons on a regular basis, at least once a year.

(4) In establishing and implementing its risk management system, the company shall give due consideration to the interests of its employees, employees within its supply chains and those who may otherwise be directly affected in a protected legal position by the economic actions of the company or by the economic actions of a company in its supply chains.

11.4 § 5 Risk analysis

(1) As part of risk management, the enterprise shall conduct an appropriate risk analysis in accordance with paragraphs 2 to 4 to identify the human rights and environmental risks in its own business operations and those of its direct suppliers. In cases where an enterprise has engaged in an abusive arrangement of the immediate supplier relationship or a circumvention transaction to circumvent the due diligence requirements with respect to the immediate

supplier, an indirect supplier shall be deemed to be an immediate supplier.

(2) The identified human rights and environmental risks shall be appropriately weighted and prioritized. In particular, the criteria set out in Section 3 (2) shall be decisive in this respect.

(3) The company must ensure that the results of the risk analysis are communicated internally to the relevant decision-makers, such as the Management Board or the Purchasing Department.

11.5 § 6 Preventive Measures

(1) If a company notes a risk in the course of a risk analysis in accordance with Section 5, it shall immediately take appropriate preventive measures in accordance with Paragraphs 2 to 4.

(2) The company shall issue a policy statement on its human rights strategy. The company management shall issue the policy statement. The policy statement shall contain at least the following elements of a human rights strategy of the enterprise:

- A description of the procedure by which the company fulfills its obligations under Section 4 (1), Section 5 (1), Section 6 (3) to (5), and Sections 7 to 10,

- The priority human rights and environmental risks identified for the company on the basis of the risk analysis, and

- The determination, based on the risk analysis, of the human rights and environmental expectations that the company has for its employees and suppliers in the supply chain.

(3) The company must embed appropriate prevention measures in its own business operations, in particular:

- Implementing the human rights strategy outlined in the Policy Statement in relevant business operations,
- The development and implementation of appropriate procurement strategies and purchasing practices that prevent or minimize identified risks,
- The implementation of training in relevant business operations,
- The implementation of risk-based control measures that verify compliance with the human rights strategy contained in the policy statement in its own business area

(4) The company must anchor appropriate preventive measures with respect to a direct supplier, in particular:

- The consideration of human rights and environmental expectations when selecting a direct supplier,
- Contractually assuring an immediate supplier that it will comply with the human rights-related and environmental expectations required by the company's management and adequately address them along the supply chain,
- The implementation of training and education to enforce the contractual assurances of the immediate supplier, as set forth in number 2,
- The agreement of appropriate contractual monitoring mechanisms and their risk-based implementation to verify compliance with the human rights strategy at the immediate supplier.

(5) The effectiveness of the preventive measures shall be reviewed once a year and on an ad hoc basis if the company must expect a significantly changed or significantly expanded risk situation in its own business area or at the direct

supplier, for example, due to the introduction of new products, projects or a new business area. Findings from the processing of notices pursuant to § 8 (1) shall be taken into account. The measures shall be updated without delay as required.

The risk analysis must be carried out once a year as well as on an ad hoc basis if the company must expect a significantly changed or significantly expanded risk situation in the supply chain, for example, due to the introduction of new products, projects or a new business field. Findings from the processing of notices pursuant to § 8 (1) shall be taken into account.

11.6 § 7 Remedial Measures

(1) If the company notes that the violation of a human rights-related or an environmental obligation has already occurred or is imminent in its own business area or at a direct supplier, it shall immediately take appropriate remedial action to prevent or end this violation or to minimize the extent of the violation. § Section 5 (1) sentence 2 shall apply accordingly. In the company's own business area in Germany, the remedial action must lead to an end of the infringement. In the company's own business area abroad and in its own business area pursuant to Section 2 (6) sentence 3, the remedial action must generally lead to termination of the infringement.

(2) If the violation of a human rights-related or an environmental obligation at a direct supplier is such that the company cannot end it in the foreseeable future, it must immediately draw up and implement a concept to end or minimize it. The concept must contain a concrete time schedule. In preparing and implementing the concept, the following measures in particular shall be considered:

1. The joint development and implementation of a plan to terminate or minimize the violation with the company by which the violation is caused,

2. Joining forces with other companies in industry initiatives and industry standards to increase the ability to influence the violator,

3. A temporary suspension of the business relationship during risk mitigation efforts.

(3) Termination of a business relationship is only required if.

1. The violation of a protected legal position or an environmental obligation is judged to be very serious,

2. The implementation of the measures worked out in the concept does not result in Corrective Action after the expiry of the time specified in the concept,

3. The company has no other mitigating means at its disposal and an increase in its ability to exert influence does not appear to be promising.

4. The mere fact that a state has not ratified one of the conventions listed in the Annex to this Act or has not implemented it in its national law shall not result in an obligation to terminate the business relationship. The second sentence shall not affect restrictions on foreign trade imposed by or on the basis of federal law, European Union law or international law.

(4) The effectiveness of the remedial measures shall be reviewed once a year and on an ad hoc basis if the company must expect a significantly changed or significantly expanded risk situation in its own business area or at the direct supplier, for example, due to the introduction of new products, projects or a new business area. Findings from the processing of notices pursuant to § 8 (1) shall be taken into account. The measures shall be updated without delay as required.

11.7 § 8 Complaints Procedure

(5) The company shall ensure that an appropriate internal complaints procedure is in place in accordance with Paragraphs 2 to 4. The complaints procedure enables persons to point out human rights and environmental risks as well as violations of human rights-related or environmental obligations that have arisen as a result of the economic actions of a company in its own business area or of a direct supplier. The whistleblowers must be given confirmation that the information has been received. The persons entrusted by the company with the implementation of the procedure shall discuss the facts with the whistleblowers. They may offer a procedure for amicable settlement. Companies may instead participate in an appropriate external complaint procedure, provided it meets the following criteria.

(6) The company shall establish rules of procedure in text form, which shall be publicly accessible.

(7) The persons entrusted by the company with the implementation of the procedure must offer a guarantee of impartiality, in particular, they must be independent and not bound by instructions. They shall be bound to secrecy.

(8) The company must make clear and comprehensible information on accessibility and responsibility and on the implementation of the complaints procedure publicly available in a suitable manner. The complaints procedure must be accessible to potential participants, maintain confidentiality of identity and ensure effective protection against disadvantage or punishment on the basis of a complaint.

12

Table of Figures

www.ingramcontent.com/pod-product-compliance
Lightning Source LLC
Chambersburg PA
CBHW081820200326
41597CB00023B/4324